Buddhism
and
American Thinkers

BUDDHISM
AND
AMERICAN THINKERS

EDITED BY

KENNETH K. INADA AND NOLAN P. JACOBSON

State University of New York Press
ALBANY

Published by
State University of New York Press, Albany

© 1984 State University of New York

All rights reserved

Printed in the United States of America

For information, address State University of New York Press, State University Plaza, Albany, N.Y., 12246

Library of Congress Cataloging in Publication Data
Main entry under title:

Buddhism and American thinkers.

Includes bibliographical references and index.
1. Philosophy, Buddhist—Addresses, essays, lectures. 2. Philosophy, American—20th century—Addresses, essays, lectures. 3. Philosophy, Comparative—Addresses, essays, lectures. 4. Buddhism—Doctrines—Addresses, essays, lectures. I. Inada, Kenneth K. II. Jacobson, Nolan Pliny.
B162.B83   1983   181'.043'0973   83-409
ISBN 0-87395-753-9
ISBN 0-87395-754-7 (pbk.)

10 9 8 7 6 5 4 3 2 1

Contents

177914

vi   *Contents*

Introduction

The Buddhist-American
Encounter in Philosophy

The essays presented here constitute one kind of answer to the question as to why Buddhism, the last of the great Asiatic schools of thought to reach American shores, has been moving ever deeper into the very substratum of American philosophy, with the result that we find concepts of the self in William James which could have been written by a Buddhist, a concept of Peace in Whitehead which has been called an American formulation of Nirvāna, the ideas of personal identity which were first formulated in the Buddhist "no-soul, no-substance" perspective more than two thousand years ago, and the remark of Charles Hartshorne in this volume that he "was already almost a Buddhist without knowing it long before I had read much about Buddhism or had any habit of relating my thinking to that tradition." Hartshorne acknowledges that for many years he has been "trying to make Buddhism a factor in American thinking." Charles Peirce had preceded him in this, a fact that Hartshorne wishes to emphasize in the title of his essay, the term "Buddhisto-Christian Religion" coming straight from Peirce.

Without knowing it at the time, Hartshorne was already working in ideas that constitute a common core of Buddhist and American philosophy before he took up his work as graduate assistant to Whitehead in the mid-twenties. Ideas out of the broad Buddhist background had actually been a part of the Western tradition for so long that no one would normally have been conscious of his Buddhist origin, and, as Donald Lach says, "no systematic analysis of these materials has so far been undertaken."[1] Examples abound. "Point-instants" or "fleeting moments" (khanavāda) travel sub rosa the Eurasian continent from Buddhist beginnings, become a part of the Neo-Confucian synthesis of Chu Hsi (A.D. 1130–1200), and enter the Leibnizian "Monadology" which conceives the world as a vast organism of unextended atomic point-instants, each enjoying its own distinctive "windowless" existence. While this is no longer Buddhism, neither is it the distinctive European tradition.

Whatever the specific influences, the Buddhist-American encounter is a matter of record. The essays presented here are an attempt to advance the dialogue which may be said to have commenced in earnest during the last decade of the preceding century in the writing of Charles Sanders Peirce, certain essays of Josiah Royce, the publication in 1896 of Henry Clarke Warren's *Buddhism in Translations* (still available in paperback), the World Columbian Exposition at Chicago in 1893 with the appearance of Dharmapala, Shaku Soyen and Daisetz T. Suzuki, and the decisive influence of Asia upon numerous people of prominence, such as, James Whistler in art, Frank Lloyd Wright in architecture, Paul Carus in philosophy, and many others like Henry Adams, grandson of the sixth American president, who for a time was a member of a Buddhist group in Boston.

Thousands of books, journal articles, and doctoral dissertations are appearing from year to year, written out of many different philosophical persuasions—Existentialism, Idealism, Linguistic Analysis, Marxism, Phenomenology—and by people with expertise in all the major areas of philosophy—aesthetics, comparative philosophy, epistemology, ethics, logic, philosophy of science, social philosophy, metaphysics and religion. For the most part, however, the essays in the present anthology are, in McDaniel's words, "an effort to use Whiteheadian categories of thought as aids in interpreting the Buddhist orientation to life."

All of this discussion is American philosophy's endeavor to take the non-Western world into account, and it is but a natural part of the move toward Asia among an intellectual elite; during the last twenty-five years membership has increased from a mere five hundred to more than ten thousand members in professional societies which include the Association for Asian Studies, American Oriental Society, International Association of Buddhist Studies, Society for Asian and Comparative Philosophy, International Society for Chinese Philosophy, and many others. Midway in the present century, as Inada reminds us, investigations of Buddhism became more serious, lost the atmosphere of faddishness, freed themselves from damaging misconceptions stemming from Schopenhauer, emerged from European tendencies to see Buddhism as a mere extension of Hinduism, and with academic interchange accelerating between Asia and the West, reached a position where they are now capable of asking the truly generic Buddhist questions. The present collection of essays is devoted to these questions, such as, human suffering *(dukkha),* its nature, sources and cure;

the social nature of reality and its creative freedom from any deterministic law; how reality is experienced and known; the nature of compassionate love; the problem of personal identity; and what one Japanese philosopher recently called "the aesthetic nature of man's ultimate concern," a concern which for Buddhism in all its forms is best left unconceptualized since the point is not to catch it in a linguistic and conceptual net but to awaken, to become more fully alive, compassionate and whole.

Whitehead was vaguely aware that his "philosophy of organism" bore certain similarities to Indian and Chinese thought,[2] but the most striking example of the penetration of Buddhist philosophy into the American tradition is found in the nonverbal, tacit level of Whitehead's Buddhist affinities, all the more remarkable because of its testimony to the subtle nature of Buddhism's encounter with the West. Certain explicit similarities with Buddhist perspectives, on which a considerable literature is now available, appear in the work of Whitehead who not only knew very little about Buddhism, but was largely mistaken in the little that he knew. Inada has elsewhere explored these errors at length.[3]

As compared to Whitehead, for example, Buddhism tries harder to cure man's unconscious tendency to mistake intellectual structure for clarity of thought and to manifest a surprising degree of emotional clinging to conceptual structures and certain persisting conclusions regarding our experience in the world. Buddhism in this respect is one of the world's great efforts toward a truly self-corrective community. The present dialogue, therefore, has some potential for generating among Americans the possibility for cultural renewal. The essay by Jacobson, indeed, suggests that the polarized conflicts of races, ethnic groups and social classes can be assigned to the back burner only as individuals become more capable of celebrating the creative fullness of their experience in and for itself. Nakamura makes this clearer in his discussion of a Buddhist concept of equality, based in the fact that persons, regardless of racial, ethnic and other groupings, individually "reflect the entire universe of existence," the poor no less than the rich, the politically powerful no more than the weak.

Of all the great philosophical orientations to life, none has been more critical and analytical, none more militantly concerned than Buddhism to probe the strange world of deep-rooted presuppositions and assumptive forms. Buddhism is the tradition most single-mindedly committed to penetrating the menagerie of cultural form down to the movement of reality itself as it is self-evidently given in everyday experience. Buddhism is first in its systematic attempt to be free *from* what Wittgenstein called "the tyranny of language," and to be free *for* what Einstein called "new creations of the mind."

Writing out of a critical, but nonetheless Whiteheadian orientation, David Hall argues that it is the primary responsibility of philosophy to free contemporary men and women from their cultural fragmentation, as victims of the constrictive and censorious ways in which existing forms of art, morality, science and religion destroy the unbroken wholeness of our cultural experience when it is examined in depth. This is why Hall has given his essay the title, "The Width of Civilized Experience." Hall discusses three philosophers of science—Needham, Northrop, and Whitehead—and concludes that of the three, Whitehead offers the most suitable bridge to Oriental thought and provides the needed basis for comparative understandings because of his emphasis upon the process character of reality. The major contrast, Hall argues, is not between East and West, but between substance- and process-centered philosophies. Substance philosophers remain enthralled with the form-enduring character of ideas, while the real world as we experience it is "form-transcending." At this point Hall faults Whitehead for not "widening" our civilized experience of religion, accusing him of being "half-hearted" and "somewhat apologetic" in his obvious intention of freeing his readers from the Western tendency to mistake an intellectually clear concept of God for the object of religious experience. In religion, as elsewhere, process philosophy sees the real world as "form-transcending."

Neville also finds Whitehead defective or ambiguous at this point and argues that one of the great services of Buddhism to the American scene stems from its call to abandon inadequate conceptions of the divine and develop a more convincing and profound ontological vision.

The analysis in which David Hume celebrated the firm roots of intellect in feeling has its parallel in the history of thought only in the equally radical anti-substantialism of the Buddhist legacy. Hume found the self a spurious notion built out of the whole cloth of supposititious learnings.

In both Peirce and Whitehead, likewise, we find brilliant elaborations of the life of feeling as the aesthetic foundation of life, with logic and ethics occupying the upper floors of the edifice of knowledge. "Concepts," Hall writes here, "are abstractions which must continually be referred to the concrete experiencings from which they derive." He continues, "The aim of philosophical abstractions is to heighten the experience of what is real." Hartshorne agrees. "One thing we need to learn from the Buddhists," he says, "is the importance of nonconceptual, nontheoretical apprehension of reality." In the Buddhist tradition such statements are consistent with the most rigorous concerns of logic, historical fact elaborated in Richard Chi's discussion of Dignāga (c. A.D. 400–485), the founder of Buddhist logic, whose contributions to truth functions antedated the modern Western versions by over fourteen hundred years, in what Chi calls "the earliest logical tabulation in history." The closing words of this introductory essay, which come from Hartshorne's contribution to the collection, should be read in the context of this long and creative Buddhist preoccupation with logic. No American metaphysician has ever exceeded Hartshorne's confidence and competence in logic.

Buddhism is a philosophy of internal criticism, using concepts to extend the range and vividness of awareness, to loosen the grip of dominant conceptual metaphors and compulsive unconscious drives, and to deepen attention to the rich qualitative flow people discover in their own experience as they free themselves from their culture-bound caves. For Buddhism, the function of philosophic thought is to foster the ultimate momentum of life in its concrete, harmonious flow. In the second century A.D., Nāgārjuna was saying that the sense of the real in man needs to be put on its own. As Ramanan expands, "to set free the sense of the real from its moorings in abstractions constitutes the chief-most mission of the farer on the Middle Way."[4]

Philosophers of both Buddhist and American traditions have been distrustful of language, unwilling to take it at face value, wary of seeking reality in the realm of what is most indefinite and abstract. When expressed in systems of belief passively accepted and adhered to by any individual or group, thinking loses its distinctive power to discern and communicate the unfamiliar, the unconventional, the strange and novel forms of to-getherness, which Whitehead called "the really real things whose inter-connections and individual characters constitute the universe."[5] "The real world is the aesthetically breath-taking colorful world," as Northrop writes, "and it is no longer necessary to infer non-aesthetic material and mental substances whose interaction has the effect of throwing our emotive, aesthetic selves and the other directly sensed concrete facts of experience out of nature, as unreal phantasms."[6] The balanced intensity of experience needs no philosophical or theological support; it has positive structure and value in and for itself; it is, indeed, the fundamental chaos-transcending point in the creative advance of life.

This kind of focus on language is equally at home in both Buddhist and American philosophy. In its ordinary dictionary form, language is unconfessedly provincial and parochial, reflecting the metaphors of a particular self-encapsulated culture. While we cannot leap free from our dictionaries, linguistic analysis has a role to play where men and women in the American experience are involved in new dialogues at the interface between radically different racial, ethnic, ancestral cultures and traditions which no linguistic technology has any license to forbid. The possibility, acceptable to Buddhism from its beginnings, has come to puzzle and confound: the more our understanding grows, the less familiar, the stranger and more beautiful the world becomes. Neville shows us here the ontological basis for the Buddhist experience of enlightenment. No bond is stronger between Buddhism and American philosophy than this vision and its accompanying sophistication regarding language.

The deepest American encounter with Buddhism, however, makes its appearance with Peirce, who related his convictions more specifically to Buddhism than anyone had previously done. For Peirce, as for Buddhism in all its forms—Theravāda, Mahāyāna, Vajrayāna, Zen and others—there is no determinate actuality nor autonomous being or entity at the center of things; the world is ruled neither by the relentless sway of omnipotent matter nor by blind chance.

The world that exists is the result of the *non*existence of any independent substance, any ultimate, unanalyzable entity. What is universal and concrete is the self-surpassing process and unbroken wholeness of a world in whose microscopic "point instants" the instantaneous joy and compassion are generated and felt in all who have not turned away. The oceans are not deep enough to contain the tears of billions of men and women who have been too distracted by compulsive drives and one-sided cultural perspectives to relate themselves richly to the harmony of life-enjoying-life in their own experience. Human failure and personal defeat are here the sources of what Buddhism means by suffering *(dukkha)*. Buddhism is a long effort to help individuals seek their sense of worth and participation in the original centers of relatedness, in the qualitative fullness of the passing forms of a world.

This "fullness of existence," the term offered by Inada, has been discussed under the category of *śūnyatā*, where he attempts to relate it to the American experience. *Śūnyatā*, Inada says, is the single most important category of Mahāyāna Buddhism, lying at the experiential basis which ends in the Bodhisattva Ideal with its extensive fellow-feeling and compassion.

In many ways this is the exact opposite of the Aristotelian-Thomist position, where the exhaustive actualization of all possible being and value is contributed by none of the world's creatures since the forms of reality were given from the first day of creation. Nāgārjuna put the Buddhist position in the most provocative way: "At nowhere and at no time can entities ever exist by originating out of themselves, from others, from both (self-other), or from the lack of causes."[7] Neville's essay explores in considerable detail some of the ways in which this proposition is being interpreted by American process philosophers.

The whole of Buddhist thought is permeated with this Heraclitean perspective. Like Whiteheadian thinking, Buddhism is a philosophy of process. "One easily understands, therefore," Neville writes, "the enthusiasm with which process philosophers applaud the Western discovery of Buddhist philosophy as a commanding metaphysical vision of process whose profoundest technical expressions are themselves ancient." In this connection, one of the major aims of Hartshorne's essay is to stress the one-way, asymmetrical and creative freedom of the process, a matter left ambiguous in most forms of Buddhism. A quote from Peirce puts the point with precision: "The indeterminate future becomes the determinate past." The process of creative becoming perpetually resynthesizes its previous productions, and the emergent synthesis is what production ultimately is. "So far as becoming is a process of creative synthesis," Hartshorne writes, "the future in its concreteness is only possible, rather than necessary." Various interpretations of Buddhism, Fa-tsang's (A.D. 643–712) in particular, appear to deny Peirce's point in favor of a symmetrical interpretation of future and past. Neville's essay offers alternatives for the clarification of Buddhism's long ambiguity on the issue.

In his comparisons of Western interpreters of nirvāṇa, Welbon has argued that "creativity pervades both the way and the goal of Buddhism. To ignore its presence would be to imperil any attempt to understand the Buddhist nirvāṇa and to overlook the one unambiguous distinction between Buddhism and Hinduism in most of its forms."[8] Persisting analysis of what is actually going on in the stillness of the passing moment reveals a creativity infinitely productive of actualities, each fleeting instant participating in the determination of the actual world. Buddhism is the first philosophy to perceive reality as a creative social process. Herbert Guenther remarks succinctly that creative forces are all that exist—in all the interrelated forms of the world, in flowers that bloom, in the birdsong of the passing moment.[9] The logical opposite of creativity for Buddhism is not its absence. The opposite of creativity is suffering (dukkha). The initial essay by Hartshorne calls for a "Buddhisto-Christian" dialogue to understand the real nature of this creativity in man and the rest of nature. Hartshorne believes that the creativity in this process form "can do more to explain reality than any other belief." The dialogue of Buddhism and American thinkers on this point has the potential for producing those "physicians of culture" anticipated by Nietzsche a century ago, healing encapsulation by outworn and exhausted ideas and assumptions.

Inada finds much in the American experience that is creative in this Buddhist sense—free, flexible, resilient, accommodative, integrative and whole. Polarities both positive and negative, with their attendant tensions and sufferings, are awakening the deep consciousness of the average American. "He is being tempted to be more sensitive and probe deeper into the dynamics of his experience." Writing from a Buddhist point of view, Inada finds the conditions unique here for something approximating a *śūnyatā*-oriented experience. Qualities such as freedom, freshness, movement, vision and vividness are realizable "only because of the 'empty' nature in which plural elements are thrashed out, assimilated and embodied in the on-going process"—a process which is through and through pragmatic and self-perpetuating.

As a philosopher dominated by theological concerns, Henry Nelson Wieman found the ontological sources of these cultural dynamics in a creative interchange that is never within the control of man because it transforms human experience with new meanings which individuals have no way of seeking in advance and integrates new meanings with old, expanding man's appreciable world and shared community in ways that are likewise without a human handle. The vivid qualities of an individual's original experience emerge in a creative interchange that transforms the world. Wieman sees that within the cultural context of the American experience, men and women have arrived at a point in human history where interdependence has become so intimate and so coercive between different regions, social levels, and areas of experience that this creative interchange must be viewed as the ontological imperative "if the story of man is to continue." Wieman appears to have joined much of John Dewey's pragmatism and empiricism with Whitehead's insights as a process philosopher, particularly in his stress upon the prehensiveness, responsiveness, vivid feeling, and "novel forms of togetherness" which everyone and everything share in greater or lesser degree.

Wieman is a different kind of Buddhist, to be sure, but the way he connects creativity as dynamic process with the joy or suffering that attend its freer or more restricted operation, finds obvious echoes in what Welbon, Guenther, Hartshorne and Inada have said. Wieman also shares with Buddhism, as David Miller's essay shows, a strong suspicion of those forms and formulations of large-scale religious organizations which have the potential for becoming one of the major evils in human life. Religion should be directed, Miller argues, not to its own time-honored beliefs, but to what is found in practice and controlled inquiry that transforms human life "as it cannot transform itself." There is such a thing as a "religion of mental illness" where beliefs are held so compulsively that they resist all modification by evidence or reason. Every Buddhist over the centuries would agree. Wieman's analysis of human suffering is probably closer to Buddhism than any other American thinker up to the present time. As Miller emphasizes, both Buddhism and Wieman argue that disorientation from the flow of felt creativity is the fundamental source of the suffering that is too deep for tears.

Nothing is more obvious, then, than the fact—entirely consistent with Buddhist assumptions—that Buddhism in the matrix of American thought changes through the encounter. Neville argues that Buddhist and process thinkers can and do learn from one another. Complications sometimes interfere with the Buddhist-Whiteheadian dialogue simply because both Buddhism and Whitehead are interpreted in different ways, some of which represent intellectual commitments that are very deep-rooted in each tradition.

American philosophy is becoming increasingly populated by men and women who agree with the way Koller characterizes the aim of Buddhism—"to enable a person to participate directly in reality without the intermediaries of false selves, desires, and ambitions estranging him from reality."[10] This selflessness of Buddhism, its denial of any substantial self as a receptacle for whatever happens in an individual's experience *(anattā)*, is the necessary counterpart of *pratītya-samutpāda (paṭicca-samuppāda)*, the doctrine regarding the "conditioned genesis" (the term preferred by K.N. Jayatilleke) or "interrelational existence" (the explicit title of Nakamura's contribution to this anthology). According to Inada, Nāgārjuna's greatest contribution was to spell out in concrete terms the equation of this doctrine with *śūnyatā*.

Egocentric motivations, in Buddhism, mean "writhing in delusion."[11] It was Whitehead's judgment of William James that his greatness lay in his ability to generate among his readers a more receptive mind and heart, a readiness "to find significance in new experiences from whatever direction they might come,"[12] a quality that may be called a truly Buddhist feature in William James. Gordon Allport is one among many who have seen this "Buddhism" in James: "There is, he thinks, no such thing as a substantive self distinguishable from the sum total, or stream, of experiences. Each moment of consciousness, he says, appropriates each previous moment, and the knower is thus somehow embedded in what is known."[13] Not every Buddhist could state the position more clearly than this. The "self" is a high level abstraction from the concreteness of life's qualitative flow; or as Peirce put it, the "self" is an inference from the self-active experience in the momentary present.

In the present anthology, Jacobson and McDaniel have written the most thoroughgoing analysis of this astigmatic self. McDaniel draws on Whiteheadian and Zen writings, particularly Hisamatsu and Nishitani, to carry out the Buddhist analysis of the literal selflessness of reality, and the enlightenment that issues when experience is successfully freed from the self's almost inexhaustible restraints. "Any concept of the self," Jacobson writes, "is an effort to express the limitlessness of human experience within the limits of language, and as such it is apt to be surrounded with the atmosphere of absurdity." Jacobson's analysis endeavors to trace the illusions and compulsiveness of the "self" to three primary sources—language, social motivations, and unconscious compulsive drives, which have been the subject of considerable clinical psychological research. The major terrors of the modern nation, he believes—their pretensions to autonomy and service of the well-being and security of their citizens—are rooted ultimately in what Buddhism sees as a supposititious self.

Jacobson draws upon Peirce and Nishida to show that real personal identity is found by analyzing our experience with greater freedom and depth, penetrating into the aesthetic process of qualitative enrichment (what Nishida called "pure experience") that characterizes our everyday life. Beneath the forms of conscious awareness we find the microprocesses of millions of moments called *khaṇa-vāda* in the Buddhist tradition, events that are the conveyorbelt for the quality that directs each human career. Individuals do not suffer peaceably the loss of this qualitative enrichment from their experience. Jacobson argues that both Buddhist and other philosophers must bear more responsibility for helping their fellow-creatures to discover what is really real in their experience; consequently, philosophers are more responsible than anyone else for the future of mankind.

There is no element in the universe capable of pure privacy—this follows from the doctrine of *pratītya-samutpāda,* the conditioned genesis or interrelatedness of things. High energy physics is confirming the point today; there are no mutually independent contemporaries; only at the human level is the need to awaken and become aware of the interrelatedness an urgent fact of life. "The universe," as Whitehead put it, "is through and through interdependent."[14] Rigorous efforts are needed to awaken to this unyielding fact; its discovery in our personal experience is capable of making our thoughts at home in the world after long alienation (which Marjorie Grene credits Whitehead with doing the most to bring to an end).[15]

Metaphysical confusion and malignancies have been analyzed in great detail by Buddhists for twenty-five hundred years. Individuals become disoriented from what is really real by the pursuit of wealth and power, the strains to sustain permanent elements in life-process *(bhavāsava)*, by sensual and sexual gratifications *(kāmāsava)*, and by the self-deluding and self-justifying machinations that keep people from discovering what is going on in their experience *(ditthāsava* and *avijjāsava)*. It is the thesis of Jacobson that these distortions of selfhood constitute the major obstacle to the continuation of human civilization. The endangered future, he argues, resides in the fact that there is no limit to the ways in which self-deluded, self-encapsulated individuals can be wrong about the nature of reality.

These introductory remarks have lead us to the American doorstep, which may be closer than we think to some of the major features of the Buddhist orientation. It would be a grievous oversight, however, not to stress that the point of Buddhism has never been, and is not now, to acquire a new interpretation of the world; the point, Marx and Buddhism agree, is to change it. The Buddhist legacy is an effort to think, not *about* the world, but *in* the world, as part of its organic self-surpassing wholeness. Thinking exhibits in its most intense form the propensity in man for becoming self-illuminating, centering life in the sensitive underside of the mind beneath all the overlays and widening the range of life's rich, qualitative flow.

Understanding concepts does not resolve the problem of suffering; the chief concern of the Buddha was most decisively to end the pain, and this is not achieved by putting the head of the metaphysician (even a "process" philosopher) on top of our own. Instead of being satisifed with inventing a new philosophical system, the Buddhist legacy leads directly to the more fully awakened mind. One concept is better than another if it enables an individual to penetrate to the balanced intensities of experience. Buddhism may be taken as symbolizing the effort of countless millions of people to break the strands of compulsive behavior and socially coercive authoritarian systems, that through meditation and analysis[16] they may explore the unspoken and unspeakable flow of life itself. As Hartshorne's essay put it, "we need something additional to any theory. We even need a certain freedom from theory. Life at its best is no mere application of theory, however good. We need to feel as well as think in good ways.

We need to be artists in living, creative as well as kindly. Buddhist meditation has this as its purpose."

Kenneth K. Inada
Nolan P. Jacobson

Buffalo, New York
Adel, Georgia

Prefatory Remarks to Charles Hartshorne's Essay

The leading process philosopher of our time intimately divulges his own awakening to the fundamentals of process thought. It is at once a refreshing and engaging essay which exhibits how a great mind very early on encountered different religious and philosophical views and how quickly he formed his own position on the reality of things. It is the realization that any perspective based on self-interest and substance is fundamentally limiting and doomed. Hartshorne finds sufficient confirmation and corroboration of his views in the later Harvard writings of Whitehead.

What is more dramatic and revealing is his admission of an affinity to a form of Buddhist view, especially the Mahāyāna type, even before he had seriously read anything substantial on Buddhism. It was indeed a happy coincidence. Hartshorne's keen perceptivity prompted him to conclude that events arise in an asymmetric and social matrix, i.e., the present with the past and the future as a potential with the present. He strongly senses such a matrix in the Buddhist doctrines of no-soul, dependent origination, and Bodhisattvahood.

Finally, Hartshorne calls for a Buddhisto-Christian dialogue to understand the real nature of creativity in man and the rest of nature. His essay thus creates a framework in which other essays in this volume could most profitably be read and suggests possible lines of development in the dialogue.

1

Toward a Buddhisto-Christian Religion

Charles Hartshorne

Buddhism in both its northern or Mahāyāna and its southern or Theravāda forms differs from most other ways of thinking, especially those common in the West, in several respects. So far as two of these differences are concerned, I was already almost a Buddhist without knowing it long before I had read much about Buddhism or had any habit of relating my thinking to that tradition.

First of all, in the West the favorite theory of motivation has been that self-interest is the universal principle, and interest in others only a special case or corollary of sufficiently enlightened self-interest. About my nineteenth year I was for a time a convinced proponent of this deceptively simple doctrine; but within a year or so I had, once for all, thought my way out of it. At the time (1917–1918) I was not at college (but was an orderly in an army hospital) and was not thinking particularly of any philosopher. I may have been unconsciously influenced by having read, some months before, Royce's great essay on community in his *Problem of Christianity*. I may also have read what he writes about Buddhism in that book. I was certainly influenced by St. Paul's "We are members one of another," which Royce quotes or which came up in Rufus Jone's course at Haverford in which we discussed Royce's book.

Secondly, in the West change has been analyzed as a succession of properties "in" an identical something, individual or "substance." The "same" entity loses some properties while gaining others. I do not recall having ever very definitely accepted this analysis, or having made it a problem, before encountering the early version of Whitehead's analysis of reality in terms of events (in his *Concept of Nature*). That was several years after leaving the army and after I had begun definitely to study the history of philosophy at Harvard. Whitehead's view in that book was no special shock to me. It fitted such intuitions as I had concerning experience and nature. Presumably, reading Heraclitus, Hume, Bergson, James and perhaps still others had helped prepare me for a "process" view.

Rather early in my studies at Harvard I wrote an essay in which I reached the conclusion that "the self is its own maker." This doctrine, which I later found in Whitehead, Jules Lequier and Sartre, makes little sense if a self is a single entity with more or less changing properties. For then that entity is already in existence in the first moment of its career, and any self-creation must be accomplished in that first moment.

The two Western doctrines mentioned above belong together. If selfhood is an identity through change, then self-concern is an identity relation. A concerned for A. But then also altruism is a nonidentity relation, A concerned for B. And if identity is what justifies concern, nonidentity should imply lack of concern. Thus, it becomes necessary for a moralist to try to prove a dependence of one's own welfare upon that of others. We love ourselves because we are ourselves, and we love others because we need the others for our own good.

In 1917–1918, before I had had any course in philosophy (Jones's course was in Christian doctrine), I came to see that identity does not explain motivation. There is no such relation as A loving A, where the two occurrences of A refer to simply one and the same entity. I also saw that if identity did explain motivation, it would not be almost impossible (and it is almost impossible) to get people to act simply for their own long-run welfare. Nothing is commoner than preferring present pleasure, pleasure in coming seconds, hours, weeks, to the long-run happiness of the very "same" self. Substantial identity is not the secret of motivation.

It is false that we can feel love (sympathy, compassion, admiration, concern) for others only by connecting their welfare to our own future advantage. Nor does love become more rational by being so connected. "You are important in my eyes only because I need you, whereas I am important because I am I" is the quintessence of irrationality. For one thing, you may live forty or more years after I am dead. Our common mortality ought, it then seemed and still seems to me, to teach us that in the long run we are but contributions to the future of life. And "enlightened" interest is the long-run interest, is it not?

Not only my own thinking plus Whitehead confirmed me in these convictions; the writings of Peirce that Paul Weiss and I edited supported similar views. And Peirce related them more specifically than Whitehead did to the Buddhist tradition. His expression "Buddhisto-Christian" is one of his acknowledgments of this relationship. Whitehead once put an essential point in Buddhism (without any reference, perhaps even in his own mind, to that tradition) by saying to the one class of his I ever took part in (because I was assisting him to grade papers): "I sometimes think that all modern immorality is caused by the Aristotelian theory of substance." Virtually all Buddhists have affirmed the "no soul, no substance" doctrine, partly because the substance view tends to encourage self-interest theories of motivation, and also because it is a crude analysis of our experience of change. Genetic identity is so far from sheer logical identity and is such an obscure and one-sided notion that to force the phenomena of volition and emotion to conform to it is a grave error. Think of the difference between a person in dreamless sleep and a person wide awake and thinking vigorously. The first is as unconscious as a tree (Fechner would have said, more so). Or think of the difference between a four-month embryo or a new-born infant, and a normal adult. Any "sameness" that spans such gigantic differences is a very limited sameness. Why should such a relative and paradoxical notion be allowed to tyrannize over our basic response to life?

Part of the confusion arises as follows. Your or my career, meaning the event-sequence (a very complex combination of event-sequences in fact) making up your or my bodily-mental history, is clearly distinguishable from the career of any other human person. What is quite false, however, is that the complex of events making up such a career is all "in" something already in existence at or before birth. To conceive what existed at my or your birth, one must abstract from everything that has happened since then. Ergo, the identical self is a very abstract entity. The concrete self that has my present thoughts "in" it only come to be with those thoughts. Why is it that this simple truth has escaped almost everyone but Buddhists and a few Western philosophers?

Substance thinking confuses the abstract and the concrete. Of course, something of me was there when I was born. But the "I" that now thinks about Buddhism was not that something, and that babyish something can never think those thoughts. As a contemporary Spanish philosopher has written, "I am always the same person, but not the same thing," i.e., the same concrete actuality. The sameness of the person is an abstract sameness. Concretely we are numerically new each moment.

Motivation depends on much more concrete matters than substantial identity. The universal principle is not interest by and in oneself as always the same entity, nor is it interest in others as always others; it is interest by the self of the given moment (the total self-active experience of that moment) in other experiences or selves, some momentary or nearly so, and others more abstract and enduring. Some of these other selves will be continuations of the career to which the present self belongs, others will not. (That distinction is not always very relevant.) Life is interested in life, experience in experience. Self-interest is a special case of this universal principle, altruism is another case. Not enlightened self-interest, but simply enlightened interest is the ultimate principle of right motivation, where enlightened means sufficiently future-regarding and sufficiently comprehensive of others' as well as one's own future. Love of persons and oneself as one person among others is more basic and rational than love of self simply as self. All awareness has an element of sympathy, and self-concern is a special, somewhat narrow form of this sympathy. One feels one's past feelings and sympathetically imagines one's future feelings; similar relations to others' past or future feelings explain the possibility of altruism. Without sympathy there would be no human self and no social others. It's all a question of how far we generalize the scope of our sympathy at each moment for life at other moments, whether your life or mine is, from the rational point of view, secondary. Not to see this is, as the Buddhists say, "writhing in delusion." (If this language seems too strong, turn on your television set or read the newspaper.)

No matter how enlightened, self-interest is not ultimate, and no self-interest theory should be taken literally as such. What is to be taken more nearly literally is the injunction, "Love your neighbor *as* yourself." How can this be done if the one love is simply identity and the other simply nonidentity? Of course, some relative differences are insuperable between self-sympathy and sympathy for others, but to absolutize the differences, as so many have done, and regard this absolutization as the criterion of rationality, is indeed lamentable. To be entirely rational is to love the whole ongoing universe, and oneself and one's future only as items in that universe—for that is to see things as they are. We are but pebbles on the cosmic beach.

As Niebuhr used to say, each animal tends to see itself as the center of the world; but reason tells us that none of us is that center. To make self-centeredness, no matter how subtly or ingeniously, *the* first principle is a strange misuse of reason. It is time religious people faced the "as yourself" idea and made up their minds about it. By good luck I reached this point before I was twenty-one and have never seen any reason to go back to my previous adherence to a self-interest doctrine.

Return to that prison? Never! It ties the present self to an absolute obligation to the future fortunes of that enduring (i.e., abstract) self and forbids it to admit any but an indirect obligation to anything beyond those fortunes. It imprisons the concrete momentary self in favor of the abstract self. (This is the real "prison of individuality" the Buddhists speak of. I am not aware, however, of any Buddhist writer who has given that phrase quite the explicit context I have just given it.)

I find in my own writings that I was speaking confidently about Buddhism as early as 1937, but I then stressed my differences from the religion more than my agreements with it. In 1957, I obtained a Fulbright grant to lecture in Kyoto University in the Spring and early Summer of 1958. I did this partly because of an interest in Buddhism, partly because of my awareness of the intelligence of Japanese scholars, and partly for still other reasons. To prepare for meeting Japanese philosophers, I read T. R. V. Murti's *The Central Philosophy of Buddhism.* I had already read Stcherbatsky's *The Central Conception of Buddhism.* These two books, together with the Russian author's *Buddhist Logic,* sum up the philosophic content of the Buddhist tradition.

The negative side of the doctrine is indicated most briefly in the "no soul, no substance" doctrine. A Japanese interpreter replied to a Westerner's "You mean to say you deny the immortality of the soul!" with, "In the first place, there's no soul." From Plato to Kant, Western thinkers tend to make the idea of a soul and the belief in experiences of one's own after death two aspects of one truth. So the Japanese reply was to the point. (That he may have himself believed in reincarnation is another and in my opinion philosophically irrelevant matter.) Every moment each of us is a new entity—indeed, taking the body into account, many new entities. It follows that identity is not the key to motivation, love is not reducible to intelligent self-regard, and the very concept of self as it functions in this phrase is unintelligent, ambiguous or partly illusory in principle. Not substance but "dependent origination," causality properly understood, is the key to motivation. Self-love, taken as *the* motive, is an arbitrary fixation upon a mere portion of the past origins and future consequences of the concrete, now experiencing self.

Buddhism, in one aspect, is among the most radical pluralisms of all. Heraclitus' "You cannot step twice into the same river" is, as Whitehead once put it, an understatement. Neither you nor the river is known to be but a single entity, even at a single moment. In a second many events occur; there are no simply lasting single entities. Phenomenal reality is complex beyond our easy comprehension. Becoming, origination—Is not alteration of entities already there? It is perpetual production of new entities, which, having become, are forthwith superseded by still newer ones. Creation and supersession by further creation is what concrete reality is. To set one's heart on the given moment and its entitites is vain; and, since the individual person is but a limited sequence of closely related moments with some persistent characteristics, to view it as the measure of value for one's decisions is equally vain. Nothing short of Something universal to the process of dependent origination can be the measure of value for a nondeluded person. What is this Something?

Southern Buddhism at this point seems to adhere to Gautama's reported agnosticism. Not cosmology nor theology is needed, but only the means of escape from suffering. And these means are ways of overcoming self-centeredness and attachment to the temporary as though it were or could be permanent. Compassion for all, without attachment to any specific goals, whether for self or for others, seems to be the recommended program.

Of course there is paradox here. The goal is to have no goals, or is it to have no goals except that of transcending all goal-seeking? "Escape from suffering" is negative. There must be a positive side. For the sake of elements of joy, we can all bear considerable suffering. How can the Buddhist prove that this is irrational? What is the positive side of the salvation that the Buddhist monk is seeking? Is it happiness? But by the doctrine, any state of happiness is temporary. And whose happiness? Is the goal self-centered after all?

The Mahāyāna Bodhisattva ideal, not wholly absent from the Theravāda, is to renounce complete salvation for self until it is attained by all, not just all persons, but even all creatures. Thus the goal of having no goal is indefinitely (infinitely?) postponed.

Northern Buddhism also differed in its ontology. It produced a theory of universal oneness in the universal plurality of created-superseded entities. This is the theory known in the West as that of universally internal relations, or the theory of universal interdependence. It was close to the surface in Spinoza, explicit in Hegel and some other idealists. This is an extreme monism as the final meaning of a philosophy which seems initially an extreme pluralism. By omitting this final meaning, the Theravāda remains, as Stcherbatsky said, an extreme pluralism, while the Mahāyāna is an extreme monism. In this splitting into two contrary extremes, I see evidence that the famous "Middle Way" of Northern Buddhism was not quite what it claimed to be. The golden mean was not found.

Nāgārjuna, an early founder of the Mahāyāna, argued that neither a metaphysics of universal interdependence nor one of universal independence can be made rationally intelligible. We cannot understand relations if they are exclusively internal, nor can we understand them if they are exclusively external. Bradley, many centuries later (independently, I presume) repeats the reasoning. Suppose (as I believe) that they were both right so far, what follows? They replied, what follows is that the truth about relations transcends discursive thought and can only be possessed by those whose meditation or intuition carries them beyond the rationally statable. I say that this, as it stands, is a non sequitur for relations may be internal in some cases and external in others, internal to some terms but also external to some. Neither Nāgārjuna nor Bradley gave any clear objections to such a middle ground position; indeed, neither of them formulated it clearly.

Later, in the Hua-yen tradition of China, Fa-tsang, in spite of the warnings of Nāgārjuna, affirmed universal interdependence. All events implicate their causes, and all causes, their effects; each entity depends on all others. It has no self-being and in itself is nothing, *śunyatā,* emptiness. Only all-process is real. But, as Nāgārjuna rightly held, this conception defies logic. The whole is nothing without the parts, the parts nothing without the whole. If we do not know everything we know nothing. And we cannot know everything. Explanation is circular. Neither parts nor whole are identifiable.

There is here in the history of Buddhism a large scale exhibition of a truth which I seem to be the first philosopher to see clearly. This is that symmetrical conceptions, such as the concepts of past, present, and future bound together in a mutually dependent order, are always partial truths, never the whole truth, and reliance upon such conceptions generates dilemmas, the escape from which requires giving up both of two opposite extremes in favor of a middle position that takes asymmetry as primary. If in every case of A related to B, the relation is internal to or constitutive of both A and B, that is extreme monism. It makes every dependence symmetrical, or a case of interdependence, and it generates incurable paradox. If, in every case of A related to B, the relation is external to both A and B, that is extreme pluralism. It makes independence symmetrical. It, too, generates paradox. For now, we have three entities, A, B, and the relation. And we are saying either that these three entities have a further relation such that the first relation, call it R, relates A to B (implying a vicious regress repeating the same problem), or that relations ae super-entities able to contain their terms. Neither way can one make sense out of the theory.

The solution is to suppose that the primary relations are those of one-way dependence-independence. A may depend on B but not B on A. Examples are easy to furnish. We depend on George Washington for his contribution to our American life; he did not depend on us, and we make no contribution to his life. A tree depends on the seed from which it sprang, but that seed could have been all that it once was and yet never have sprouted and grown into the tree. Earlier events may be independent of later ones but not vice versa; causes may be independent of effects but not vice versa. To carry through this line of thought, we must renounce all classical or strict determinism, the notion that every event has both "necessary and sufficient" conditions in preceding events. Necessary conditions, yes, but sufficient conditions, no. More subtly, "sufficient" is here ambiguous. "Sufficient to make an event of the kind that happened possible" is one meaning, and of course, it must always apply, for the impossible does not happen; but, "sufficient to make the event happen" need not apply if we are talking about previous events, for it may be the event itself that makes itself happen. Just this is creative freedom.

The very phrase "dependent origination" implies asymmetry. An event originates out of the past as its necessary condition. It does not originate out of the future as necessary condition. Washington helped to make us; we have done nothing to make him.

In medieval China, as later by Zen in Japan, the symmetrical view, incompatible with creativity, was taken. One meets it in contemporary neo-Buddhist Japanese philosophers, some of whom state it less clearly than Fa-tsang did; indeed, I could scarcely understand them until I heard a scholar in Chinese philosophy expound Fa-tsang.

In the West, determinism has had a great hold on thought. Adequate appreciation for the asymmetrical view that takes "time's arrow" seriously began with Charles Peirce. His sentence, "the indeterminate future become the determinate past," sums up this aspect. The sentence could equally well have been written by Bergson or Whitehead. When I showed Whitehead the passage, he asked me to bear witness that this was the first time (it was, I think, in 1927) that he had seen it, but it also expressed his own view. This passage, implies a dependence of later events upon earlier but *not vice versa*. Cumulative creation means that no definiteness is lost, but there are gains in definiteness with each new event. Becoming perpetually resynthesizes its previous productions, and this emergent synthesizing is what production ultimately is.

Whereas Theravāda Buddhism had seemed to say that nothing abides, since every gain becomes a subsequent loss, and Mahāyāna Buddhism seemed to say that there is neither gain nor loss but an eternal nothing which is somehow everything; process philosophy, in the Peirce-Bergson-Whitehead-Hartshorne version, says that there is real gain but no loss at all. There are, to be sure, "lost opportunities," and these can be genuinely lost, but loss here only means, "not actualized possibilities." Once a possible event has become actual, it is an imperishable item in reality.

The preservation of actualized possibilities is partially exhibited in ordinary memory and perception. Looking into the starry heavens at night, we can see where various stars were years in the past. To perceive is to look into the past, not the present, state of things. Such past states are still real; otherwise, how could they be items in our awareness? Remembering our own past feelings, we still to some extent possess them. The possession is a severely qualified one for much is no longer accessible to our consciousness. Here is one reason why most process philosophers have been theists, because they can form an idea of deity as the unqualified memory-and-perception of all past happenings. In this way, all actualized values are "objectively immortal" in "the consequent nature of God," i.e., in God as aware of what goes on in the world.

In this view we have something that is lacking both in Buddhism and in classical Western theology. Buddhism never very clearly accepted the asymmetrical view of cumulative becoming and tended, even in the Mahāyāna, to lack a clear conception of deity; while Western classical theism, by treating God as timeless or immutable, implied that for God, the totality of events is embraced once and for all in God's omniscience. For process philosophy there can be no such thing as "*the* totality of events," for each moment there are additional events. There is always a *de facto* totality, but no sooner is it referred to than it is already out of date and there is a richer totality, even for God.

Does this view imply God's knowledge is defective, that he is ignorant of part of the truth? Not at all. As the Socinian theologians (neglected in this respect by the rest of the world for over three centuries now) had argued, it is not ignorance to know only those truths that really obtain. And no truth obtains until the thing that it is true of exists. What you or I tomorrow decide to do is not a definite reality until the decision is "*made.*" It is not a possible item in eternal knowledge, for events do not exist eternally.

There can be truths about the future, but only so far as there are causal necessities or probabilities for the future, given what has already happened. And so far as becoming is creative, a process of emergent synthesis, the future in its concreteness is only possible (probability is a special form of possibility) rather than necessary. This is the truth, and the truth is what God knows. The Socinians had already, in the 17th Century, made all this clear enough—with only one limitation: they did not generalize creativity so that it applied to every creature as such, but (so far as I know) limited it to God and humankind. Otherwise they were process philosophers in principle by having an asymmetrical view of becoming and by conceiving

God as acquiring novel content from the novelities in the world. It was Lequier, aware to some extent of the Socinians, who spelled out the implication: we create not only something of our own being, but also something of God's being. Our decisions, he said, "make a spot in the Absolute." (Personally, I deplore using the term absolute as synonym for divine, since the doctrine Lequier and I accept implies a genuinely relative aspect of deity as well as the absolute aspect. But Lequier is essentially aware of the point and is being deliberately paradoxical.)

It does seem to me that Western metaphysics, now at last, is in a position to find important ground with Buddhism, the most international of Far Eastern religions, and from a global perspective, we can do better than either East or West was able to do in previous centuries. More than any other belief, it seems, the belief in Supreme creativity, inspiring, guiding and everlastingly cherishing lesser forms of creativity, can do more to explain reality and give us ideals.

It is perhaps necessary to add that the universalizing of creativity radically alters the classical "problem of evil" by implying that the concept of omnipotence which generates the problem is a pseudoconception. Omnipotence does not mean a greater degree of power than God has, it is only a self-contradiction. On the one hand, it takes God as supremely powerful; on the other hand, it implies that only God has any power at all, if power means decision-making capacity. To be supremely powerful in a world of lesser powers is one idea, and it makes a certain sense; to be the only power in a vacuum of power is quite another idea, and it does not make sense. The *supremely* creative being, in this sense *the* Creator, cannot be the *only* creative being. The world is not simply and unilaterally "made" by God: in details it is made by the nondivine lesser creators. In ordinary language we speak of *making* decisions, and these decisions have consequences by which we literally make some aspects of the world.

First of all, we make ourselves as parts of the world. Lequier said it for all time: "Thou hast created me creator of myself." Whitehead's "self-created creature" is a (probably unconscious) repetition of Lequier, except that Whitehead is speaking of any and every creature, not just human persons. This is an important generalization, but Lequier furnished the idea to be generalized. It was also in Philo Judaeus, but he did not use the expression "self-created," nor clearly admit that our creating reacts on God, alters his concrete reality.

The West has finally produced a full generalization of the old East-West idea of free creation. This is a cultural event of potentially great importance. That it has happened is only beginning to be noticed. Tom,

Dick and Harry have heard of the death of God, but not yet of the view that the God who died was never the living God that people were trying to worship, but only a blunder made by theologians who fell into an oversimplified view of the content of religious experience. Supreme Creativity, inspiring and guiding a world of lesser forms of creativity, is only now being clearly envisaged. What it can do for human life remains to be seen. As a human conception it is struggling to be born. It is too soon to declare its decease.

However this may be, it is time to take the "no soul, no substance" doctrine of Buddhism into account in our philosophical and religious reflections, together with the ideal of universal compassion and overcoming of self-centeredness. It is time also to see that if we had taken seriously the Western religious doctrine of loving the other *as* onself, we might have discovered that both self-concern and other-concern are forms of one principle and that principle is neither simple substantial identity nor simple nonidentity. All regard for the future transcends the present actual self having the concern, but this actual self will in all cases become a contribution to the future of life and its value: it is through this "objective immortality" alone that self can have any permanent significance. If self-interest means the present self willing its own objective immortality, then self-interest is indeed an ultimate aspect of motivation. But regard for the *future* welfare of the abstract or enduring self, John Smith or Mary Miller, is secondary and derivative—merely one way, and in the long run not the final way, to optimally immortalize the present self. Self-interest in this ultimate sense has *nothing* to do with selfishness as used in ordinary language and in most philosophies of substance.

These matters are subtle, but lack of intellect is hardly the only reason many go astray in thinking about them. Our animal self-centeredness tends to bias us in favor of theories that erect self-regard into a rational necessity or criterion of rightness. Here, too, Buddhism is helpful. Its thinkers tried mightily and with brilliant theorizing to overcome this animal limitation. We should strive to learn from them.

We might begin with the importance of nonconceptual, nontheoretical apprehension of reality. In this respect, my account so far has been onesided. (I am helped to see this by the writings of Nolan Jacobson.) I have written as though the merit of Buddhism was that it had the right theory of the self and of motivation, but that what we need is a still better theory. We need, however, something additional to any theory. We even need a certain freedom from theory (insofar as Nāgārjuna's criticisms of conceptual understanding are justified). Self-interest and substance theories are hampering, they imprison us, but life at its best is no mere application of theory, however good. Maeterlinck said, "it is necessary to live naively." We have to respond to situations always more complex than we can understand, and we have to respond with more than understanding. We need to feel as well as think in good ways. We need to be artists in living, creative as well as kindly. Buddhist meditation has this as its purpose.

I have also been one-sided in stressing the long-run contributions we make in each present moment to the future of life, but I did not mean merely utilitarian contributions, whether growing food for others to eat or writing books for others to read. I meant also what we add to the world's beauty by the harmony and intensity of our own present inner life. As a theist I hold, with Robert Browning, that no matter how hidden from others such beauty may be, if it occurs, it will have been taken into the divine life once for all.

Prefatory Remarks to David Hall's Essay

It is the primary responsibility of philosophy, Hall argues, to free contemporary men and women from their cultural fragmentation by making them more conscious of the way art, morality, science, religion and philosophy have become specialized, censorial, constrictive and destructive to the unbroken wholeness of our cultural experience. The enrichment of Anglo-European cultural resources with what Hall calls "novel evidences found within Oriental cultures" is a responsibility of our "philosophical elite." Joseph Needham and F. S. C. Northrop point the way, but Whitehead's philosophy provides a basis for correcting the errors of the two great pioneers, suggesting an epistemic correlation of aesthetic and theoretic components of experience, which Northrop's Kantian tendencies obscure, and a creative imagination offering the elements of novelty and self-creativity which Needham's high regard for Leibniz leaves unclear. Hall draws upon Chinese thought and culture in its Buddhist and Taoist expressions to provide "the novel evidences" needed to enrich our own cultural sensorium and provide a broader and richer set of philosophic understandings. It is the function of Whitehead's philosophy, speaking in our own ancestral tongue, to enable us to perceive what these Chinese evidences mean. Creative aesthetic events possessed of freedom, transience and novel purpose—the "mystical" Whitehead presently overshadowed by Whitehead the neo-classical theologian—are philosophical notions that heighten the sense of what is real in its most intense and harmonious concreteness. Creative engagement with alternative cultures awakens the civilizing activity of philosophy from its provincial slumbers.

2

The Width of Civilized Experience: Comparative Philosophy and the Pursuit of Evidence

David L. Hall

> The chief danger to philosophy is
> narrowness in the selection of
> evidence.
> —A. N. Whitehead

Quite apart from its intrinsic interest, the increased communication between Anglo-European and Oriental cultures over the last two or three decades is of greatest pragmatic significance. The ultimate consequence of this inter-cultural communication will undoubtedly be the recognition of common values and the sense of sharing a common destiny. Of greater immediate significance, however, is the mutual recognition and articulation of those important differences which suggest the presence of untapped sources of cultural enrichment. My concern in the following pages is to suggest why Anglo-European culture ought, and how it can, pursue some of the distinctively novel resources to be found in Oriental thought and culture.

The primary processes in Anglo-European culture concerned with the formulation of facts and the appreciation of values are grounded in the cultural interests of art, morality, science, religion and philosophy. Organized into a pattern of sense-making activities these interests constitute a *cultural sensorium* defining both the potentialities and limitations of individual and social existence within intellectual culture. The absence or derogation of a cultural sense is as threatening to our cultural well-being as is the failure of a physiological sense to our organic wholeness.

That there are these five principal sources of cultural experience is a consequence of the perspectival limitations we have, in fact, placed upon our manner of being in the world. Data are felt as efficacious in the constitution of an individual act of experiencing in accordance with three distinct modes of perspectival abstraction—viz., as immediately felt, as a finite field of discriminated data the components of which are differentially relevant to the emergent efficacy of the individual experience, and finally, as a putatively infinite, undiscriminated Totality. As immediate, the experienced data are referred to the private psychological field of the experiencing entity and felt solely in terms of their *suchness* or just-so-ness. As proximate, the focus is upon the relevance of selected data to the individual in the act of self-constitution. The unlimited context of experiencing promotes the contrast between the individual as finite detail and the Totality of the experienceable world. These three perspectives provide the foundation of the cultural interests of art, morality, and religion, respectively.

We discover the grounding of the interests of science and philosophy at the more sophisticated level of conscious perception and knowledge. The scientific enterprise requires a contrast of the world as consciously perceived with that same world as causally efficacious in the constitution of the act of experiencing. Science extends beyond simply the causal interpretation of nature construed as the terminus of sense perception. It includes the logical and systematic interpretations of aesthetic, moral and religious experience as well. The "scientific" interpretation of these interests is obedient to the criterion of truth as an expression of logical consistency and rational coherence. The intuitions and activities of the artist, the ethical agent, and the religious virtuoso, experienced in terms of the distinctive perspectival limitation of each, constitute these interests in their most direct form. Speculative philosophy, the generic mode of the philosophic enterprise, is to be understood as *scientia scientiarum;* it is primarily concerned with the organization into a coherent whole of the evidences of the four alternative cultural interests. Like science, it involves the formal interpretation of experience at the level of consciousness and concepts, but unlike the specialized sciences, it aspires to complete generality in its treatment of evidence.

The primary value of this somewhat vague and abstract typology is that it permits us to raise the very complex question of the sources of cultural evidence in a manageable, but nonetheless reasonably intelligent, manner.

Obviously these various modes of experiencing interpenetrate. The relative degree of distinctness involved in the differentiation of types of cultural interest is largely due to their articulation at the level of conscious praxis. A most significant consequence of this differentiation, however achieved, is that the various cultural activities grounded upon these modes of interest can lead to serious conflicts of a value-orientation. It is perhaps not even possible to achieve a co-ordination of all of the principal cultural aims without relegating one or more of them to a decidedly ancillary role. Keats' roseate line, "Beauty is Truth, Truth Beauty . . . ," though possessed of poetic beauty, is decidedly untrue as a generalization because of the existence of terribly blunt truths which challenge all aesthetic feeling, not to mention the phantasmal beauty of certain products of an undisciplined imagination, having no grounding beyond the flux of present circumstance. Nor is truth or beauty always *good*. Value is the outcome of limitation, and that limitation, with respect to any given attainment of value, leads to the exclusion of alternative values almost of necessity. Conflicts of beauty and goodness named by the phenomenon of censorship, or of truth and importance illustrated by the pedantic sense, or of holiness and goodness, evident in the activities of some among our saints and mystics, speak all too clearly of the possible disharmonies resulting from the overly specialized production of value.

For a variety of reasons which cannot be detailed in this context,[1] the scientific and moral interests, and the imaginative visions of the world attendant upon them, have dominated our cultural sensorium from very nearly the beginning of our intellectual culture. That is to say, the theoretical concern for truth as naming a direct relation between Appearance and Reality, on the one hand, and a desire for the control of praxis so as to maximize its efficacy in the achieving of individual and social goods, on the other, have provided the fundamental principles for the organization of our cultural aims and interests. A consequence of this fact is that the remaining cultural interests, and the imaginative modes present within them, have been construed in terms of exigencies in the relations of persons and nature (the scientific relation) and persons and society (the moral relation).

The various interactions of these two dominant interests have significantly influenced the character of our cultural milieu. The scientific influence on the moral interest is evidenced in the development of ethical and political visions expressing the fundamental meanings of individual and social activities in terms of principles of conduct. The intuitive feelings which are the putative ground of ethical behavior are rendered ancillary and, more often than not, held suspect. Ethical and political behavior of a spontaneous sort is eschewed in favor of actions which either appeal to normative principles or are grounded in a prudent assessment of possible consequences. The moral interest impinges upon the scientific through its insistence that scientists concern themselves with the short-term achievement of specific personal and social goods. The instrumental rationality of science is stressed above its theorial, visionary character. The mutual disciplining of the scientific and moral interests is primarily responsible for the ubiquity of technological imperatives in our contemporary society. As a complex of processes, modern technology constitutes a wedding of the scientific and moral interests. Substantively considered our technological ambience is increasingly identified as both *physis* and *praxis* and, as such, may be seen to constitute both our "natural" and moral environs.

The intersection of the moral and scientific interests in the phenomenon of technological society has seriously challenged the continued efficacy of art, religion and philosophy. In our highly organized society, the scientific concern leads to the intense specialization of cultural interests which, in turn, requires the relative detachment of these interests one from the other. The moral interest further compounds this situation by influencing artists either to perform socially relevant activities or to accede to the relegation of their profession to the status of a ghettoized superfluity. The moral interest combines with the scientific to influence theological inquiry away from the direct confrontation of mystical and sacred aspects of religious sensibility and toward the essentially apologetic function of legitimizing specific forms of doctrinal and institutional commitments. Under these conditions philosophy cannot but wither, detached as it is from the richness and complexity of its cultural resources. Philosophers must then have recourse to their traditional strategies of retreat: retreat into the analysis of isolated problems of language, logic, science, or the narrower forms of social praxis, or into the development of speculative visions which arise not from the concrete problematics of contemporary culture, but from the defects of other philosophic systems, or from the murky depths of Being-Itself.

Just as is the case with our physiological senses, each of the specific interests comprising our cultural sensorium provides a distinct perspective on the world of experience. Thus the dominance of the scientific and moral sensibilities has determined that we see the world in terms of the stabilities and regularities required by moral norms and scientific laws. The ephemeral world of aesthetic experience, wherein the only norm or law is that which celebrates the decay of realized perfections and the re-emergence of novelty, is not one of our most fundamental concerns. Nor do we sufficiently appreciate the world of the mystic which, grounded in the experience of an interpenetrating unity, defies rational articulation. It is a sad but firm fact of our culture—interludes of untoward forms of irrational romanticism to the contrary notwithstanding—that neither the evidences of art nor of religion are given proper attention.

In Anglo-European culture, particularly since the Renaissance, art has tended to be evaluated in terms of the moral thematics of its specific social context, and the technical rules employed in its realization. We discover or invent principles which will best enable us to *understand* art. But the desire for understanding (not to mention the instrumental definition of "understanding" most often presupposed) precludes the most direct confrontation of the aesthetic enterprise. The tendentious silliness of most "art for art's sake" theories, which attempt to affirm a pure aestheticism in opposition to the ethical and technical appraisals of art, is due to the absence in our culture of an aesthetic ontology in accordance with which we may defend the view that "a work of art is its own excuse for being." The uniqueness and just-so-ness of aesthetic objects is impossible to grasp if we have recourse to *principles* as the sole criteria of evaluation. But we are no better off if we yield to an irrational revolt from principles which leads to no important alternative vision.

The religious sensibility is no less a victim of our cultural imbalance. After we remove the strictly ethical injunctions which are thought to be entailed by our paradigmatic religious experiences, and after we have deleted all of the arguments and demonstrations informing our developed theological tradition, what remains? Apparently we have spent the greater part of our energies articulating the characteristics of the Primary Religious Object, constructing subtle arguments aimed at demonstrating His existence, and affirming this Ultimate Being to be the authoritative source of those moral norms which stabilize our social existence. The *mysterium tremendum,* the holiness character of existence, the sense of mystical identity, the sacred aura surrounding certain places, events and personages—these are more often celebrated by mystical poets than by dogmatic theologians. Both religion and art actually seem bizarre in our culture almost precisely to the extent that they are approached on their own terms, apart from the ethical and rational criteria which serve to organize and discipline our social and cultural activities.

In despite of all the signal achievements this specialization has permitted, the dominance of moral and scientific interests has occasioned a significantly narrowed and dulled complex of cultural experiences. An important cultural imperative, therefore, is the endeavor to release the aesthetic and religious sensibilities from the constraints of the scientific and moral impulses. It is in performing this task that philosophy can lay claim to its own distinctive importance. For it is primarily the responsibility of the contemporary philosopher of culture to articulate the importance of aesthetic and religious interests, thus enriching our cultural expressions by enabling us to draw upon the width of civilized experience.

The enrichment of Anglo-European cultural resources through the pursuit of novel evidences found within Oriental culture is one of the more pressing of the responsibilities of our philosophical elite. The urgency of the task ought not, however, blind us to its intrinsic difficulty. It is essential that we develop *rigorous comparative methodologies* which permit responsible access to the philosophic riches to be discovered beyond our cultural boundaries. But we must allow our comparative generalizations to be disciplined by those analytic and exegetical endeavors which interpret *alternative cultural evidences in situ*. For it is through such endeavors that the variety and complexity of each culture is to be recognized and the specific similarities and differences in cultural expression are to be uncovered. We can never remain content, however, with piecemeal interpretations of this or that aspect of an exoteric culture. Adequate comparative methodologies require recourse to more general understandings which render specialized insights meaningful within the broadest possible contexts.

Obviously there is something of the problem of the chicken and the egg here. We cannot understand another culture until we have a language and a schema allowing translation into a cultural idiom appropriate to our understanding, but we cannot develop such a schema in a satisfactory form until we have sufficient understanding of the similarities and differences illustrated by the exoteric culture. We ought not, of course, yield to the Kipling Fallacy, the presumption that "East" and "West" represent two monolithic cultures facing one another across an unbridgeable chasm. The only reasonable response to the difficulties that intercultural translations represent is to recognize that the development of a comparative methodology is an extended process of tentative and pragmatic endeavors which only gradually may approach philosophic adequacy.

Though comparative philosophy is still in its infancy, we have made some progress in articulating the relationships of Oriental and Western thought and culture. And though we should not claim too much for our comparative endeavors since they still have the heavy-handedness of mere first attempts, we are apparently at least beginning to see where the real issues lie. Some years ago, F. S. C. Northrop developed a comparative methodology, claiming that the basis of the comparison of Eastern and Western cultures was to be found in the emphasis of the former on "concepts by intuition" and the latter's employment of "concepts by postulation." Philosophers from both sides of the cultural chasm found this comparison fruitful. Its primary advantage was that it highlighted the Anglo-European concern with the development of scientific concepts in contrast to the aesthetic orientation of the East. The *Kantian epistemology* on which this scheme was loosely based led, however, to its being criticized by Anglo-European philosophers because it reinforced only one possible interpretation of scientific development in the West—that which divorced postulated concepts from any experiential or empirical ground. Oriental philosophes have criticized Northrop's comparative schema and it is criticized in some quarters of comparative philosophy today, but his comparative methodology was quite influential in promoting precisely the kind of philosophical discussions which have permitted us to increase the subtlety of our cross-cultural understandings.

An alternative to Northrop's scheme was provided by Joseph Needham in his magnificent multi-volume work, *Science and Civilization in China*. In specific criticism of Northrop's distinction between Eastern and Western modes of apprehending nature, Needham claims:

> There is no good reason for denying to the theories of the *Yin* and the *Yang,* or the Five Elements, the same status of proto-scientific hypotheses as can be claimed by the schools of the pre-Socratic and other Greek schools. What went wrong with Chinese science was . . . that no Renaissance awoke it from its "empirical slumbers."[2]

In contrast with Northrop's distinction between Western scientific and Eastern aesthetic culture, Needham assumes the scientific mode of apprehension to be a fundamental way of seeing things and then looks for social and economic contingencies in Chinese culture to account for its failure to fully develop the scientific sensibility. For Needham, the most viable relation between Western and specifically Chinese culture would obtain if the Chinese had recourse to Western scientific methodology to articulate their proto-scientific hypotheses, and if the West had looked to the organismic conception of Nature developed in Chinese thought as a means of overcoming the limitations of the mechanistic and atomistic structures of Western science.

Between them, Northrop and Needham provide speculative models for comparative philosophy, one epistemic, the other cosmological, which are extremely fruitful if approached tentatively and pragmatically. Moreover, the specific contributions of Northrop and Needham to the development of comparative methodologies can be increased if they are seen in the light of yet another suggestive insight—that drawn from the philosophy of A. N. Whitehead. Ironically, what may initially seem to be a fundamental limitation of Whitehead's thought regarding the construction of a comparative scheme—the fact that he had little first-hand knowledge of Oriental culture—turns out to be a major virtue. Whitehead's thinking lacks any of the artificiality which attends any studied attempt to build a bridge between East and West. The fortunate coincidence of his philosophic interests with those of contemporary comparative philosophers is grounded, as we shall see, in a *vision of the world which underlies both the epistemic and cosmological concerns* of our two previously discussed methodologists.

Whitehead's philosophy emerged from a critique of the limitations of classical Western science. In *Science and the Modern World* he sought to trace the rise and fall of the scientific paradigm, "how it attains its triumphs, how its influence moulds the very springs of action of mankind, and finally how at its moment of supreme success its limitations disclose themselves and call for a renewed exercise of the creative imagination."[3] Through the majestic exercise in creative imagination which formed that and later works, Whitehead incidentally provided the grounds for developing a comparative methodology which contains both epistemic and cosmological bridges to oriental culture.

Whitehead's thought provides the basis for a comparison of aesthetic and scientific modes of apprehension, which is the major thrust of Northrop's methodology, while avoiding the radical dualism between intuition and postulation that Northrop assumes. For Whitehead, the theoretic component of experience is derived from the aesthetic. Concepts are abstractions from experience. And experience must be understood as the process of self-creativity. Emphasizing the construction of concepts from out of this concrete experiencing, and their coherent organization in the development of schemes of thought, allows for the understanding of the scientific enterprise. Stressing the ongoing processes of self-creativity, and the use of concepts to evoke the sense of the immediacies of experience, provides a rationale for the interpretation of aesthetic experience.

Further, Whitehead's analysis of process as "the realization of events disposed in an interlocked community"[4] promotes the organic conception of nature which Needham finds essential in appreciating the Chinese contributions to philosophical understanding, while Whitehead's explicit familiarity with the methodologies of science, as distinct from its ontological commitments, provides the kind of tools which Needham believes the Orient ought to exploit for the development of their proto-scientific thinking. Moreover, the Whiteheadian philosophy of organism is not of the "static" variety found in Leibniz (to which Needham approvingly refers). The elements of novelty and self-creativity Whitehead employs to sustain his analysis of reality as process are missing in Leibniz due to his affirmation of a substance ontology.

Thus we can see in Whitehead's philosophy not only the basis for an epistemic correlation of aesthetic and theoretic components of experience, but the grounds for a perfected concept of nature as well. Further, each of these distinctive contributions to comparative philosophy is found in the context of a vision of reality as *process*. As we shall see, it is the process orientation of Whitehead's philosophy which renders it most suitable for comparative understandings. The Whiteheadian sensibility thus provides a bridge to Oriental thought and culture, not primarily because it offers a method for epistemic correlation between theoretic and aesthetic components of knowledge as Northrop would wish, nor mainly because it suggests the outlines of a concept of nature illustrating the consequences of scientizing the proto-scientific conceptions of Eastern organicist cosmologies as Needham claims: Whiteheadian philosophy suggests a way of crossing the great divide separating Eastern and Western cultural sensibilities principally because of its recurrence to the theme of the process character of reality as patterned by aesthetic events.

The most significant contrast in the philosophies of Oriental and Anglo-European cultures can hardly be said to obtain in any strict sense between Eastern and Western thought as a whole, rather the distinction exists between substance and process philosophies. Thus, while it is a mistake to believe that the terms "East" and "West" as broad geographical designations name monolithic cultures at variance with one another in almost every respect, it is nonetheless true that there is a significant *cultural difference* based upon the *process orientation of much of the former* and the *substance orientation of almost all of the latter*. And if we employ this comparative insight with appropriate restraint we shall find it extremely helpful in promoting intercultural communication.

Isolation the contrast between substance and process forms of philosophic vision as the distinctive focus for a comparative methodology allows us to understand the rationale both for the claim that Anglo-European culture has achieved its most important cultural expressions through the stress upon scientific and moral interests, and the further claim that the supplemental evidences of aesthetic and religious sensibilities in their purest forms may be found in the process interpretations of Oriental culture. For the contrasting commitments *to substance* and *process forms of metaphysics* are functions of differential emphases upon alternate cultural interests.

The cultural interests of science and morality depend upon the development of principles which, functioning as "universals," provide stable patternings for the interpretation of experience. It is of the character of science and ethics as normative disciplines to require that the derivative aspects of experience—i.e., the generalized or patterned constructions from experiencing—be counted as fundamental in the formation of cultural understandings. Aesthetic and mystical experience, on the other hand, are to be understood primarily in terms of the felt immediacy of an act of experiencing. Scientific and the ethical understandings promote the stable characterization of experiencing by recourse to principles; aesthetic and mystical modalities of experience celebrate the *transitoriness* of one's presence to the world.

I do not with to overstate my case. There is certainly no gainsaying the fact that each of the principal modes of cultural interest has been manifest in both substance- and process-oriented cultures. Obviously there has been a concern in Anglo-European culture to call upon "intuitions" as the ground for the development of valid principles. And the Oriental visionary of the aesthetic or mystical variety is just as obviously concerned to articulate his experiences through propositions and theories.

At the very beginning of our cultural tradition Plato acceded to the importance of aesthetic and mystical intuitions in his characterization of Eros as the desire for Beauty and in his claim that the union with the Form of Forms led one "beyond Being." But, ultimately, Plato's philosophy required the seeker of mystical union be disciplined by the science of dialectic, and the relevance of Beauty be determined by the Form of the Good as the source of normative measure. The former stricture has had profound effects upon the history of Western theology, and the latter equally profound consequences for the development of aesthetics. And though Aristotle clearly adverted to the aesthetic sensibility in his claim that the first principles of the sciences were known to be certain only through the exercise of "intuition,"[5] subsequent developments of scientific thinking in the West have increasingly led to the denial of intuitive certainty for scientific principles by some special epistemological appeal to the experience of the interpreter.[6]

With respect to Oriental culture: while it is true that the *Tao Te Ching* begins with the words, "The way that can be spoken of is not the true way," it certainly doesn't *end* there. "The Way" is described, discussed, and articulated in several thousand Chinese characters! Or, to take another example, the logical and dialectical exercises of Nāgārjuna are universally recognized as possessing an unexcelled subtlety and rigor. The Hua-yen form of Buddhism also promotes a metaphysics which aims at coherence and consistency in a manner not unlike the most systematic of Western thinkers. Clearly, too, there are ethical implications in each of the forms of Taoist and Buddhist visions. But however much recourse to principles one might find in these types of philosophy, it is always disciplined by a suspicion of propositional language and a critique of its inadequacies.

The Taoist's rebuttal to those who scorn his apparent inconsistency in speaking of "the Way that cannot truly be spoken of" is perfectly apt: "I make for you a beautiful embroidery of drakes and pass it along for your approval; I cannot, however, show you the golden needle by which it was made." And if Nāgārjuna's dialectic is impeccable, it is nevertheless a *negative* dialectic, aimed not at expressing the ultimate characteristics of things, but at demonstrating the ineffability of the "ultimate." Like the logic of a Zen (Ch'an) koan, such exercises aim not to *establish* principles as determining sources of order, but to *undermine* them. The ethical implications of these modes of thought serve not so much to organize, regulate and rationalize one's conduct with regard to one's fellows as to promote the transcendence of present circumstances and the achievement of the enlightened status of sagehood.

Even Confucianism, which unquestionably seems to represent a rational ethical system, is no exception to the dominance of aesthetic and mystical values in Chinese culture. As Herbert Fingarette has so wonderfully demonstrated in his *Confucius—The Secular as Sacred*,[7] we may properly employ *li* (the "principles" of conduct descriptive of righteous behavior) only if we are able to be *jen* (the spontaneous, harmonizing essence of action seen from the perspective of the actor himself). The morphological analysis of action in terms of *li* requires a wholly different logic than the genetic analysis of *jen*. In the Confucian tradition it is the mystical, aesthetic nature of ritual, rather than rationalized principles of conduct, that is meant to form the basis of the thought system.

Perhaps these illustrations will suffice to support the claim that the most fruitful contrast between Oriental and Anglo-European cultures involves their differential emphases upon the principal modes of cultural interest. In the discussion which follows I shall continue to concentrate on Chinese thought and culture, principally in terms of its Buddhist and Taoist expressions, in order to illustrate how the pursuit of novel evidences might permit the enrichment of our cultural sensorium and insure thereby a broader and richer set of philosophic understandings. It would, of course, require many volumes to give an adequate description of the significant contributions the aesthetic and mystical sensibilities of Chinese culture could make to Anglo-European thought and culture. In the few remaining pages of this essay I will simply allude to the distinctive character of these sensibilities and to the manner in which recourse to our indigenous process philosophies, illustrated by Whiteheadian thought, can assist us in appropriating something of these distinctive visions for the enrichment of our cultural milieu.

Classical Chinese art strikes the Anglo-European as unusual, not merely for the distinctiveness of the techniques and subject matters employed, but equally for the placement of the enterprise of aesthetic activity within its cultural milieu. There seems to be no great distinction between the practices of philosophy and art. It is as if the "quarrel between the poets and the philosophers," which Plato described at the beginnings of our intellectual culture, had never erupted in China. Artists may be philosophers, and religious virtuosi for that matter, without disrupting the character of their enterprise. We too have our scholarly and mystical artists, of course, but what seems more the exception in our own cultural milieu is a prominent characteristic of Classical Chinese culture.

If we direct our attention to the painting of the Sung Dynasty (960–1279), when the Buddhist and Taoist sensibilities had so creatively merged with the Confucian, we encounter a style of painting which, by virtue of its allusive splendor, is perhaps the very epitome of the aesthetic sense. Whether we select the expansive landscapes of the Northern Sung painter Kuo Hsi or the more restricted portrayals of Southern Sung introspective art which reached its finest expression in the Ch'an Buddhist style of Mu Ch'i, we cannot but see that something strange and wonderful indeed is to be found in the aesthetic sensibilities of Chinese artists.

Naturalistic and representational art in the West, at least since the Renaissance, has been dominated by the understanding of nature as the terminus of sense perception. Reliance upon visual perspective subordinates the aesthetic experience of the natural world to the demands of geometrical perspective and the organization of objects in three dimensional space. Whenever Western artists revise the rules of perspective they are likely to be praised or blamed for their employment of "distorted" (i.e., "unreal") spaces. The idealized landscapes of Chinese art employ a different conception of space altogether. The painter develops his subject matter in relation to three or more plane surfaces representing various distances—e.g., foreground, mid-ground, background. Each distance expresses a focal characteristic of the painting. The presentation of depth and distance in this manner confounds the sense of single focus or perspective and draws the spectator into the painting, influencing him to consider the work from a variety of points of view internal to the depicted scene itself. There is no distortion here: in shifting our focus from place to place within the painting we are moving about in aesthetic space.

Art such as we are describing attains a subtlety of nuance impossible to achieve if one begins with the presumption of the natural world as the terminus of sense perception. The narrowing strictures entailed in the necessity to conform to the presentationally immediate perception of the objects of nature means that aesthetic values are inordinately disciplined by visual perceptions. The truth-value of Sung Dynasty art, however, is emergent from an aesthetic rather than a rational order. The possible harmonies to be attained are, therefore, somewhat richer than those found in Western Renaissance and Modern forms of naturalism.[8]

A significant characteristic of the aesthetic attitude as it is represented by Sung dynasty painters is that it is no part of the painter's task to *objectify* the world. The subject of the painter is not external to him; it is internal to the artist at the moment of creation. But this internalized perspective is by no means the result of a personalizing egoism associated with the extremes of the romantics or expressionists. The world is in the painter in the same manner that the painter is in the world. And the painting must be "entered" to be enjoyed. If we view a landscape of Kuo Hsi, or an introspective work of Mu Ch'i, we immediately see that simply standing "before" the painting provides us with no privileged place. In the case of the landscape, we are asked to come inside in order to envision it from a variety of persepctives associated with the trees, mountains, waterfalls, etc. Ultimately, however, it is not the painting that is to be our concern, but the *world* which emerges from the perspective of the painting. The painting is a platform from which to view the world. Standing there we begin to understand the purpose of the artist—and of art itself. If we approach Mu Ch'i's famous painting of the "Six Per-simmons," or his idealized portrait of the poet Li Po, we are not asked to look, but to meditate. And if we do, we experience the almost unbearable vitality emergent from the relation of the painting with its world. Here, perhaps, Keats is vindicated, beauty *is* truth—not the blunt truth of conformation, but the truth of realization, of enlightenment.

The understanding of aesthetic creativity that emerges from such art as we have been discussing is strange indeed. Who is the creator? What, or whom, is created? An eighth century Chinese poet knew the solution to this puzzle:[9]

The wild geese fly across the long sky above.
Their image is reflected upon the chilly water below.
The geese do not mean to cast their images on the water;
Nor does the water mean to hold the image of the geese.

The created is unconstrained, uncaused, spontaneous. Creativity is *self-creativity*.

The difficulty we experience in fully appreciating Chinese art should sensitize us to the fact that we are not much more proficient in understanding our own art. For it is not so much the case that artists themselves have suffered from the use of rational and ethical thematics in our culture as that the *interpretations* of art within the Anglo-European cultural milieu have promoted its misunderstanding. The meaning of "creativity" in our culture is rooted in the presumedly more fundamental notion of "power." *Creatio ex nihilo*, the metaphysical paradigm for so much of our understanding of creative activity, is in fact the paradigm of all power relations. We are disposed to see creativity as production, construal, determination. As the Creator determines the existence and nature of the created object and thus establishes its dependent status, so the artist must determine the works of his hands. The further association of the concept of power with control and domination lends such an understanding of creativity as we have developed in the West a decidedly questionable cast from the explicitly aesthetic point of view.

If we are to learn the principal lesson Chinese art has to teach us— that creativity, as *self*-creativity, lies beyond the constraints of external determination—we might begin with a significant insight found in Whitehead's philosophy. Whitehead is perhaps the first major Western thinker to note the challenge to the metaphysical ultimacy of creativity consequent upon the predominantly volitional characterizations of the term. Certainly one of the more important contributions of Whitehead's philosophy is to be found in his *grounding of the notion of creativity in a shifting hierarchy of atemporal forms,* thus precluding the notion of a single-ordered world dependent for its origination upon a single instance of creativity. And by discovering the final real things to be aesthetic events possessed of freedom, transcience and novel purpose, he focused upon the *reflexive character* of *creativity* as in every instance *causa sui* and *sui generis*. The Whiteheadian sensibility provides a fundamental perspective from which to appropriate the novel aesthetic evidences of Oriental forms of process thought. Comparative philosophers ought to take the Whiteheadian sensibility seriously as a means of translating certain of the aesthetic insights of Oriental thought into a cultural idiom somewhat more approachable to Anglo-European thinkers.

The second possible contribution of Oriental culture which ought to claim our attention concerns its mystical interpretation of the religious sensibility. This is an extremely difficult subject to consider responsibly due to the inherent vagueness of the term *mysticism,* and to the attendant difficulty of distinguishing the mystical from the aesthetic sense. By mysticism, I mean the sort of *vision of the world which stresses the experience of unity of* and *with the Totality of things.* There are three principal modes of the mystical vision—what may be termed its ecstatic, enstatic and "constatic" forms.[10] We recognize these modes primarily in terms of the source or goal of the experience of union—either God (or the gods), the Soul, or Nature. In the theistic variety, God (or gods) is the occasion for an ecstatic experience in which the individual "stands outside" himself seeking union with that which otherwise transcends the soul. The *alienatio mentis a corpore* of Western mystical literature has as its motivation the God-Soul identity state in which the soul finds its rest in the Divine Presence. Enstatic mysticism reverses the locus of the experience of unity; the Divine enters the soul and establishes a peculiar immanence with it. Constatic mysticism, usually known as "Nature mysticism," involves a state in which all things "stand together" in a mutually implicative manner. For obvious reasons relating to the transcendent monotheism of classical Western theology, this form of mysticism is highly suspect. For cogent, if not equally obvious reasons, however, the constatic form of unity is the philosophically more adequate notion since it permits of specialized interpretations—abstractive emphases—suggestive of both the enstatic and ecstatic modes. In one sense or another the mystical attitude forms the essential core of all forms of religious experiencing.

Aesthetic and religious modes of experience are like reverse faces of a translucent coin. One may understand the relations of art and religion by analogy to the shifting status of figure and ground in a *gestalt.* In aesthetic experience the finite immediacy of the experiencing subject is the figure and the infinitely complex totality of experienceable data is the ground. In religious experiencing the gestalt is transformed with the undiscriminated Totality coming to the fore as figure in relation to which the experiencing subject serves as ground.

The ineffability of religious experience is a consequence of the fact that such experiencing is complete in itself. To the degree that language is used as a means of co-ordinating meaning and reference, religious experience is "meaningless" because it has no isolatable referent. Articulations of mystical experience are, in fact, *aesthetic* in character in the sense that they employ metaphor and imagery to evoke some sense of the inexhaustible depth and complexity of the experience. Most understandings of such descriptions by non-mystics are, likewise, aesthetic understandings since what is communicated is the mysterious depth of existence rather than the sense of mystical union. Sometimes aesthetic experience is said to be ineffable. Strictly speaking, however, this is a confusion, for the expressions (or, pehaps better, the allusions) of the artist do in fact communicate the inexhaustibly mysterious sense of things which is the immediate content of aesthetic experience.

Due to the intrinsic relatedness of the aesthetic and religious sensibilities, one would expect to discover mystical characteristics in art, and this is certainly true of the art we have been discussing. One has but to note the importance of voids, unfilled spaces, in Chinese painting to see that this is so. Voids suggest the transcendence of the solid and the filled. The objects in a Chinese painting are not primarily present by virtue of their extension; theirs is a *focal* presence from which they recede in all directions. Thus, they "fill" the spaces not by virtue of their density or magnitude, but simply by their allusive presence. One senses that the meaning and the being of these objects is to be found everywhere and everywhen. This effect is achieved by virtue of the evocation of a sense of what we have termed constatic unity, but which is more familiarly expressed in the Buddhist notion of *emptiness*.

Chinese Buddhist tradition provides a remarkably simple illustration of the concept of emptiness. In the T'ang Dynasty, at the close of the seventh century by Western reckoning, the Buddhist Fa-tsang was invited to the palace of Empress Wu to expound the doctrines of Hua-yen Buddhism. This he did through a demonstration involving a room whose floor, ceiling, and walls were lined with mirrors, and in the center of which he had placed a statue of the Buddha. In each mirror a Buddha image was produced, along with the images in every other mirror. Holding a small crystal ball in his hand, Fa-tsang illustrated how all the mirrors and their images were reflected in it, and it in turn was reflected in the mirrors, *ad infinitum*.[11] Not only was he attempting to illustrate the reciprocal interfusion of all things, but he wishes to evoke a sense of the dependent co-origination of each item in nature. This "dependent-arising" suggests an indifference toward the isolation of causes viewed as strictly relevant antecedents. The Totality, as an object of mystical intuition, is not to be characterized in terms of causal efficacy but, instead, in terms of mutual deference.

From the mystical perspective, Nature cannot be construed simply from the human point of view. It is *the realm of all possible construals*. It is not merely a reflection of the human mind, but a mirroring of each in all and all in each that challenges the sole validity of the human pespective. To know nature one must experience *constasy*, the sense of all things standing together in a felt unity in which, nonetheless, each item maintains its autonomy and uniqueness. The reciprocal interfusion of all things as illustrated by Fa-tsang's Hall of Mirrors provides the basis for an *understanding* of things which is not causally based. Though the Totality is the ultimate object of knowledge in each occasion of an event of knowing, it is the Totality as construed from the perspective of the ecstatic sense of the other, the enstatic sense of oneself as experienced by the other, and the constatic sense of each member standing with all things.

We must be cautious in approaching Whitehead's philosophy as a bridge to the understandings of mystical experience since the received interpretations of Whitehead's thought have tended to stress his rational theology, particularly his distinctive concept of "God." The detailed and explicit phenomenologies of religious experience in *Religion In The Making* and *Modes of Thought* have been all but ignored in favor of his complex theistic doctrines. The "mystical" Whitehead has thus been overshadowed by Whitehead the neo-classical theologian. Before we can demonstrate the value of Whiteheadian thought as a bridge to the understanding of Oriental forms of mystical religion, therefore, we must extricate the mystical elements of Whitehead's religious sensibility from his explicitly rational theology.

The clear testimony of the *philosophia perennis*, Oriental and Western, is that the apex of religious experience is the felt sense of Unity, of Oneness. For the Christian mystic this is interpreted as the God-Soul identity state. The dogmatic theology of Christianity, however, claims that "the beatific vision" is the highest form of religious experience. This beatific vision, the soul's envisagement of the Uncreated Essence of the Holy Trinity, is distinct from the God-Soul identity state in the sense that the latter, if accepted literally, would entail a challenge to the conception of the impassibility (not to mention infinity) of God, whereas the former conforms to the requirements of doctrinal theology. God, as the terminus of a mystic's intuition, is distinct from the God of theological inference. Most of the tension between the empirical claims of the mystics and the doctrinal claims of the theologians within Christianity derives from this distinction.

One would expect process philosophies in the West to side with the mystical tradition, but this has hardly been the case. Whitehead labored to revise the traditional conception of God in order that it might conform to a process view of reality, but this vision of a God whose "consequent" nature is qualified by the actualizations of the finite experiences of the temporal world, and whose "primordial" nature houses all possibility, is in the last analysis, a rather half-hearted, somewhat apologetic compromise with the rational theology of the West. This concept of God is, in one aspect, the terminus of an act of intuition, but in its primordial, nontemporal aspect God may only be inferred, as Whitehead himself recognized.[12]

Process theologians, who comprise the greater number of Whitehead's disciples, have continually stressed the concept of God as a principle of *concretion*, or the ground of *order*, rather than emphasizing the function of God as a self-creative source of novelty. Attempts to de-emphasize the importance of the concept of God have not come from those interested in the direct deliverances of intuition, but rather from those intent upon naturalizing process metaphysics.[13] The aim of this effort is not merely to construct a Whiteheadian philosophy without recourse to the concept of God; it is equally an apologetic attempt to secure Whitehead's metaphysics for the accepted canons of reason. The fate of process thought in its religious aspect has been that its rational and rationalizable components have been stressed at the expense of its intuitional foundations.

If we look at Whitehead's theology with its foundation in intuitional experience in mind we are able to realize that the notion, "God," is a concept interpretative of religious experience. To mistake the rationalized concept for the object of religious experience and belief constitutes idolatry, of course, not to mention extremely bad philosophy. It is equally important to understand that the inferred characteristics of God often have very little to do with religious sensibilities per se. "God," as a metaphysical concept, serves a number of wholly *secular* functions according to Whitehead.[14] These, of course, require articulation and analysis in a manner not altogether suitable to the needs of the religious sense. Whitehead's concept of God lacks religious availability for some precisely because of the excess baggage the notion must bear in order to provide an adequate understanding of the specifically secular functions it interprets.

Concepts, particularly *religious* concepts, are abstractions which must continually be referred to the concrete experiencings from which they derive. The aim of philosophical abstractions is to heighten the experience of what is real. The reality of religious experiencing is not to be found at the level of conscious perceptions or logical inference, but at the deepest levels of value experience. The apparent fact that the theological tradition in the West has developed toward *increasing dependence on concepts* and *doctrines as candidates for belief,* rather than toward the use *of concepts to evoke the intensities of religious experiencing,* is one of the more critical flaws in Anglo-European culture, one which ought to be corrected by recourse to mystical traditions.

We've only to consider the long list of heretics in the history of Christianity to recognize that doctrinal orthodoxy, rather than appeal to the "fruits of the spirit" evidenced in the quality of religious lives, has been the primary criterion establishing membership in the Christian Community. This is certainly an ironic fact in the light of Whitehead's apt remark, "The Buddha gave his doctrine to enlighten the world: Christ gave his life, it is for Christians to discern the doctrine."[15] For to the extent that this is true, one might initially expect the very reverse of the actual developments in Christianity and Buddhism. It is Buddhism that finds its inspiration in the concreteness of spiritual life, while Christianity has mainly sought to rationalize the intuitions of its founder. In Christianity we find a stress upon believing correctly; practical forms of the religious life have not received the same stress. Christianity "has always been a religion seeking a metaphysic, in contrast to Buddhism which is a metaphysic generating a religion."[16]

Whitehead's overly generalized, but nonetheless insightful, comparison of Christianity and Buddhism indicates the contrasting use of concepts in rational and mystical traditions. Beginning with the empirical world of appearance and developing abstractions which are thought to be explanatory of it involves the danger that we shall remain content with the abstractions themselves and thereby avoid recourse to the concrete immediacies of experience from which they actually derive. The mystical sensibility suggests rather that we begin with the acceptance of the penultimate status of the world of appearance and seek the reality that lies beneath and beyond it.

In spite of many significant differences between Whiteheadian thought and Buddhism, the process character of Whitehead's vision of the world permits him to understand the functioning of consciousness and concepts in such a manner as to promote a mystical understanding of the character and status of existing things not unlike that of the Buddhist. The fact that this is not altogether oblivious from a cursory examination of Whitehead's rational theology indicates the extent to which the metaphysical and apologetic accouterments of Whiteheadian thought have clouded his central religious insights.

Substance philosophies may remain content with the static "form-endowing" character of conceptualizations since they wish to envision the world in terms of its permanences. Process philosophies must always critize abstractions since the real world is "form-transcending." Thus the fundamental religious problematic of Whiteheadian thought is that of "perpetual perishing," and the most general expression of that problematic is "whether the process of the temporal world passes into the formation of other actualities bound together in an order in which novelty does not mean loss."[17] The answer to the religious problem is to be found in the intuition of holiness which grounds all religions. That intuition is "our sense of the value of the details for the totality."[18] The contrast of the finite individuality of transitory experiencing with the Totality of things grounds the experience of "solitariness" which is the basis for understanding the religious sensibility. Whitehead's famous phrase, "religion is what the individual does with his own solitariness,"[19] establishes the fundamentally mystical ground of his interpretation of religious sensibility. One can be *alone* in a crowd, but one may be *solitary* only when there is a sensed contrast of the finite immediacy of one's experiencing with the infinite Totality of things. In this experience one discovers the suchness, the uniqueness—and at the same time the *emptiness*—of each entity. It is only in this experience that one can envision the *ontological parity that grounds the mutually implicative relationships of all things.* And it is in this experience that one is permitted to see all things *sub specie aeternitatis,* and to sense their holiness. The continual self-transformation of the Totality into ever novel instances of unity is at once the occasion for the religious problem and, rightly viewed, the ground of its resolution.

We need more discussions of Whiteheadian philosophy which concentrate upon these mystical elements. Not only will this assist us in understanding this magnificent philosophic vision on its own terms, it will provide many comparative notions allowing us more creative access to the mystical visions of Oriental thought. For if, as I have argued in this essay, we can indeed benefit from the pursuit of novel aesthetic and religious evidences, there is little doubt that Whitehead's process philosophy can be extremely supportive of that effort.[20]

For some time now Anglo-European philosophy has suffered from a rather constricted and restrained mentality which has led it to ignore issues of general cultural importance. The urgent necessity to promote creative engagement with alternative cultures might provide precisely the kind of stimulation required to awaken contemporary philosophers from their provincial slumbers. If so, then we may hope that philosophy shall again become a civilizing and, ultimately, civilized activity.

Prefatory Remarks to Nolan Pliny Jacobson's Essay

Conditions associated with our new global interdependence are leading men and women to reexamine their experience in the world. Civilizations up to now, it is clear, suppress the inexhaustible richness of experience itself, reducing it to the limits of a linguistic system and cultural norms. If they are to survive in an interpenetrating, interdependent world, people find that they must relate themselves to their own individualized universe in new ways. Buddhism offers fresh resources in the form of perspectives congenial to this contemporary need, particularly on such questions as personal identity, the social nature of ultimate reality, and the concreteness of experience prior to all socially imposed filters and veils. Jacobson describes at length a Buddhist perspective on "the linguistic bind."

While many tributaries feed into this dialogue between Buddhism and American thinkers, there is a sharper focus in Buddhism on some issues, such as the illusory nature of the bifurcating, mutually exclusive "self" around which a dominant Western tradition supposes the events of one's life to be organized. Buddhism also places a stronger emphasis on motivation; the greatest thirst is for direct experience of the richness and harmony of life itself, instead of getting it secondhand from other people, from governments, from sacred books. Buddhism places more emphasis on suffering (dukkha) as a general consequence of turning one's back upon the creativity of life. Both Buddhist and American thinkers, however, find individual experience directly accessible to the interrelatedness of life (śūnyatā). Reality is a social process in both traditions.

3

A Buddhist Analysis of Human Experience

Nolan Pliny Jacobson

The Minister of Culture spoke in Athens recently words that express the feelings of many: "There is much sadness in our hearts," she said. An ancient Buddhist orientation echoes these words: "The oceans are not deep enough to contain the tears." Calloused by years of mass slaughter (the term is taken from the abattoir) there are many sad things in our minds today. Only a population that had lost all sense of direct and immediate contact with life could tolerate what we have all seen without going mad—thousands of innocent men, women and children murdered in Lebanon, the holocaust of Hitler's concentration camps, the more or less instantaneous death of 200,000 in the infamous case of the Bomb that drifted down by parachute to explode in Hiroshima faces fifteen minutes after the "all clear" signal had sounded, and more millions of military personnel and civilians cut off in places like Kampuchea and Vietnam, Korea and Afghanistan, and places no one had ever heard about, like Jonestown and Port Stanley. Callouses and protective shields have had to grow over the soft underside of our minds if such things were to be endured.

The daily news serves to remind us that mankind has reached some kind of unexplored barrier or frontier where the dominant ways people think about their experience and talk with one another serve more to aggravate and magnify rather than alleviate their problems. A half century ago Whitehead remarked that "mankind has entered upon a new phase; it is no good saying that you will go on in the future as you have done in the past; you can't."[1] There was a time in the world when the great struggle was to improve the material standards of consumption and to organize the structures of government so that eventually all citizens might be equal before the law, whatever their natural origin and ethnic background. There was a time when everybody knew that the struggle commanding loyalty and devotion was to lead the world in the competitive development of the satellite, the computer and microsilicon chip, the technology now comparable to the invention of the wheel. There was a time when the greatest need appeared to be to produce good technocrats, even when the world's finest graduate schools sent them back home to places like Iran with no awareness of what the mullahs and the ayatollahs had in mind.

Humanity's struggle now, if it is to survive, is to reexamine its experience in the world and come to some deeper understanding of the way civilizations reduce the vividness and range of human experience by confining it to a linguistic system and conceptual metaphors that take charge as individuals come of age. Civilizations up to now have been based upon the assumption that human beings adjust best to the ambiguous demands of everyday life by turning away from the individualized universe in its spontaneous and vivid qualitative flow, by turning their backs upon their own original concrete experience, in order to accept their lives, as it were, secondhand. The great preponderance of human energy and ingenuity has been expended in the construction and maintenance of those majestic institutions of public power—bureaucracies, hierarchies, large-scale social and ecclesiastical organizations—which suppress the intensity and richness of human experience and satisfy mankind's widely publicized need to receive, as though from a more legitimate source, the clues on how life is to be lived.

Everywhere around us we see that an archaic legacy of ancient attitudes and values define and confine people to their obsolete cultural stockades, making it next to impossible for any appreciable number to open themselves to the way their counterparts think about their experience in cultural worlds radically different from one another. People come of age in the keeping of a linguistic system which is constantly used to affirm the limits of language and experience. They are brought up complete strangers to the task of freeing life in its total ecosphere from the serpentine reductive coils that separate them from different ethnic, tribal, racial, linguistic and religious groups and thus bar them effectively from joining the community of mankind.

Men and women the world over are being prodded to take into account a new type of relationship to their own experience, new feelings regarding the presence of one another and a new sense of responsibility for the rest of nature. We live at the first time in history when little human worlds, some tracing their linguistic artifacts backward over thousands of years, can no longer confine themselves behind their self-defining cultural barriers. Hundreds of ethnic, religious and racial traditions are brewing together, in a roughly unified global crucible, the novel forms of awareness required for living together in ever more inclusive wholes, and leaving behind them the ancient claims of social classes, races, ethnic and national groups whose conflicts now threaten to bring the human adventure to an end.

An interdependent world summons the human species to abandon the cultural kindergartens in which men and women have hitherto been reared. Technology has produced instantaneous communication, and travel and migration of misplaced and displaced persons conspire together to expose everyone to ways never brought into immediate encounter until now. Ours is the first total interdependence among nations, the first time all suffer instantaneous sanctions if they try to withdraw behind high protective tariffs, export their unemployment to other nations, and try to go it alone. The flow of information has become more powerful than conventional wisdom. The knowledge explosion is winning in its struggle against the ideological mind. Against their will for the most part and without knowing exactly what is required of them, men and women are being freed from the compulsive grip of their parochial ways. Edward T. Hall summarizes all of this in the closing lines of his recent book, *Beyond Culture:* "Man must now embark on the difficult journey beyond culture; the greatest separation feat of all is when, one individual after another, we free ourselves from the grip of unconscious culture," or from what he calls "the cultural bind."[2]

"For better or worse," Joseph Needham writes, "the die is now cast, the world is one. The citizen of the world has to live with his fellow-citizens, at the ever narrowing range of the aerofoil and the radio-wave. We are living in the dawn of a new universalism which, if mankind survives the dangers attendant on control by irresponsible men of sources of power hitherto unimaginable, will unite the working peoples of all races in a community both catholic and cooperative."[3] Reviewing accounts recently published of the damage caused by the atomic bombs in Hiroshima and Nagasaki, Lewis Thomas speaks from his work in the Sloan-Kettering Cancer Center in New York: "We live today in a world densely populated by human beings living in close communication with each other all over the surface of the planet. Viewed from a certain distance the earth has the look of a single society, a community, the swarming of an intensely social species trying to figure out ways to become successfully interdependent. We obviously need, at this stage, to begin the construction of some sort of world civilization."[4]

Philosophers are now sifting through the ideas of cultures involved in this new interdependence. We are encountering new options at a time when people can no longer find freedom and richness of life within symbolic systems that have lost their ability to enthrall. We agree too much to tell people what to think, but our task has itself become somewhat clearer than before—to sharpen the alternatives and provide reasons to which different outlooks and belief systems can appeal.

In particular, American philosophers are finding in Buddhism—the oldest of the great international orientations—perspectives that deepen the dialogue a few of them have been carrying on among themselves, a dialogue that includes perspectives on such venerable philosophical issues as personal identity, suffering and alienation, the social nature of ultimate reality, love and compassion, and the concreteness of experience prior to all socially conditioned filters and veils.

The dialogue between Buddhist and American philosophers carries the highest imaginable priority from a purely historical point of view, because it parallels on the intellectual level the contemporary shift of mankind's identity *away from* the social superstructures of values and attitudes, into which a linguistic system has frozen the inexhaustible fullness of experience, *over to* experience in its fuller forms of human togetherness, experience in its individualized, unconventionalized intensities and inconceivable dimensions. Instead of laboring to maintain social superstructures of law and government, millions of men and women are discovering that experience in its unverbalized form has an inner dynamism and direction of its own, giving them a sense of being vitally and memorably alive. The dialogue between Buddhist and American philosophers parallels this historic shift.

Many streams have fed the main current of these discussions. Confucius, for example, had the Buddhist's appreciation of experience in its unsayable dimensions. There is a factor, he taught, in the rich concreteness of nonverbalized and unconventionalized experience which is not a mere sign of something beyond itself, as in the aesthetic mysticism of Meister Eckhart, and not merely transitory, but as Northrop puts it, "is ultimate, irreducible and non-transitory" summoning mankind to a life which is good because it gives expression to and is in accord with "the true nature of things."[5] Confucius taught that the more we bring into high relief the balanced richness and harmony of everyday experience, the less we are tempted to indulge ourselves in seeking out political positions of influence and power or to cling to life in any of its artificial and unnatural forms. The American Confucius, John Dewey, agreed. "The immediate existence of quality," he wrote, "is the background, the point of departure, and the regulative principle of all thinking. Language fails, not because thought fails, but because no verbal symbols can do justice to the fullness and richness of qualitative thought."[6] The editor of these Dewey essays from half a century ago, Richard Bernstein, indicated a certain cultural encapsulation with the remark that "one of the most original and basic features of Dewey's philosophy is his theory of quality," an underlying quality of indeterminateness which guides the direction of inquiry.[7]

The notion of "pure experience" was the centerpiece of Kitarō Nishida's (1870–1945) interpretation of the culture of Japan. To Japan's first philosophic genius pure experience was not identified with knowledge as in Locke, Hume and Kant, nor with the totality of man's actions and interactions as in some forms of American pragmatism.[8] Experience for Nishida is the aboriginal event of feeling the living world with no admixture of thinking or discrimination. It is the feel of life's qualitative flow which is largely hidden from the forms of understanding. "As long as we live in it, we can in no way raise even the slightest doubt about it as a whole, but being accustomed to it, continue to believe that what we are experiencing is the sole reality."[9] "Pure affective feeling is something deeply active in the living heart."[10] We maintain our sense of what is real "by reversing the direction of thinking and returning to the original condition of personal experience in a self-active, socio-historical world."[11]

Many resources and currents are available to enrich the philosophical dialogue that is taking place in America as the intellectual counterpart of the global shift *from* the form *to* the qualitative fullness of experience. Twenty-five centuries before the neo-Freudians, Karen Horney and Erich Fromm, the historical Buddha had awakened the human species to an original experience underlying conventional form, inexpressible in aesthetic richness, with a self-corrective rhythm and direction of its own. And the Buddhist tradition has always harbored a deep suspicion of large-scale social institutions, which is also a pillar of Marx's thought as he issues his call to abandon the superstructure and return to the direct feelings individuals have of one another and the rest of nature. Buddhism anticipated by twenty-five centuries Marx's summons for people to combat their tendencies to cling to theories and things which had been substituted for head and heart. The point of life in the Buddhist tradition has always been, not so much to understand the world in its changing and transitory facades, but to penetrate to what has been called "Nirvana: The Aesthetic Center of Life."[12]

American philosophy reverberates with the same emphasis upon a fullness of experience that cannot be caught in the most sensitive poetry. "Experience is not what analysis discovers but the raw material upon which analysis works."[13] "The world is felt first and only then, perhaps, known."[14] "Drops of experience, complex and interdependent" are for Whitehead the real things of which the world is finally made.[15] "What the world was to Adam on the day he opened his eyes to it, before he had drawn any distinctions, or had become conscious of his own existence—that is first, present, immediate, fresh, new, initiative, original, spontaneous, free, vivid, conscious, and evanescent."[16] "It is sufficient to go out into the air and open one's eyes to see that the world is a living spontaneity."[17] "The true empiricism," Whitehead said, "will not try to invent an absolutely different concept from that of experience, with its aspects of feeling, memory, love, freedom, and so on, in order to explain the nonhuman, but will generalize these aspects so that, though we can only dimly imagine how, they will cover all possible forms of individual existence, not only from particles to man, but even from man to God."[18] In Whitehead, the American dialogue with Buddhism is joined on the deepest level, despite the fact that he had acquired only the most superficial understanding of Buddhism and was mistaken in most of that.[19] The whole purpose of those generalizing insights we pursue in philosophy is to open our experience to more of the aesthetic richness flowing in the articulate rhythms of our bodies, where immense quantities of interconnections and feelings are stored from ages past. This Whiteheadian observation is a profoundly Buddhist perspective.

The Linguistic Bind

American philosophers have associated Whitehead with many Buddhist perspectives, but none more surprisingly Buddhist than his view that "the universe exhibits a creativity with infinite freedom," which is always in danger of being dwarfed and impoverished in human experience through a separation of language from life.[20] He criticized, for example, the specific tendency of Christianity and Buddhism to unduly shelter themselves from one another, and to be "shut up in their own forms of thought."[21] In one of the few addresses to his colleagues at Harvard that elicited very little response, he put this fear of the linguistic bind in the most general way. "For three centuries," Whitehead observed, "European learning has employed itself in a limited task. Scholars, in science and in literature, have been brilliantly successful. But they have finished that task—at least for the time. The fundamental presupposition behind learning has been that of the possession of clear ideas, as starting points for all expression and all theory. The problem has been to weave these ideas into compound structures, with the attributes of truth, or of beauty, or of moral elevation

. . . European learning was founded on the dictionary; and splendid dictionaries were produced. With the culmination of the dictionaries the epoch has ended . . . . *All the dictionaries of all the languages have failed to provide for the expression of the full human experience.*"[22] Many times Whitehead reminded himself that experience does not come in verbal phrases and that the living thought becomes frigid in the formula that expresses it.

To understand the force of Whitehead's remark, we need to remember what Robert Bellah and others have called the propensity of Western civilization[23] to be dominated by concept-oriented, definition-minded, cognitively-biased "cultures of belief."[24] Whitehead's view from philosophy, and Bellah's from sociology, have been amplified by the British anthropologist, Edmund Leach: "European learning over the past two thousand years has rested on the assumption that all the essential categories of thought had already been devised by the fifth century B.C. The art of civilized living had consisted of slotting all new experiences into Ancient Greek categories—and then we knew how to cope. This expedient has worked surprisingly well for a surprisingly long time, but it has now completely broken down. We must face up to this. Education must show quite explicitly at every level that the battery of concepts borrowed from Plato and Aristotle and the Bible, which served so well in the past, is not adequate for the twentieth century."[25]

People who come of age in the keeping of the ancestral categories and concepts are normally unaware of the power European learning has exercised in impressing upon the experience of men and women everywhere the assumptions and outlook on life which a small minority of the present world's population (almost exclusively non-pigmented and prosperous, male and middle-class) have found helpful in their drive for values. Their own consequent, subtle provincialism is as far from them as the most distant stars. They are incapable of perceiving that in covering the earth with their own half-knowledge and culture-bound conclusions, they have tended to ban from the memory of the species the intuitions and modes of awareness which multitudes of non-Europeans have experienced in the unconventionalized centers of their lives. Were Whitehead to deliver the same lecture at Harvard today, he would probably add that in its peculiar linguistic encapsulation, the West bars itself effectively from joining the community of mankind. Astronomical military expenditures are the natural result.

This essentially Buddhist perspective deserves to be taken with new seriousness if five billion people across the planet are to express their cultural differences freely in an inexhaustibly rich, interdependent world and put behind them the last form of cultural imperialism that remains—intimidation by concepts and categories formulated within the limits of one civilization and generalized to the planet at large. Western civilization has placed the emphasis on articulate speech, herding feelings into cognitive corrals, in an unacknowledged conspiracy to suppress the energizing intuitions of the widely diverse mankind.

Leading Buddhists through the centuries have always used conceptual forms to root out conflict and suffering and to penetrate into the creativity and richness of life. As people through meditation and analysis[26] become free from cultural confinement and their own individually fabricated, compulsive drives, they become for the first time capable of using concepts as instruments for widening and vivifying awareness. Some forms of Buddhist meditation focus on the meticulous handling of small items of consciousness, in themselves of no apparent significance, until, as a final cumulative impact of the analysis, the person meditating is struck silent and no longer runs out on all sides into the labyrinthine fragments of discursive thought. The end result is to restore confidence in the ability of the mind to perceive and remember what is real. The general thrust of Buddhism, therefore, is not against rational thought; it is only against culture-encapsulated and ego-centered thinking—the dominant tendencies of the contemporary world. No one reading Buddhism can miss this emphasis for example in Nāgārjuna. What he called "the claws of wisdom" are used properly to burst the established order of ignorance and of greed. Buddhist enlightenment has never meant an intellectual condition but an experience of freedom from habit-ridden schedules and routines, an awakening to the ultimate momentum of life. Buddhists are encouraged "to set free the sense of the real from its moorings in abstractions,"[27] abstractions that at present high rates of literacy provide every power structure, every dominant social class, every ethnic or racial establishment with its most effective means for the generalized control of behavior. Even the most objective scientific research has this propensity for "riveting on men a certain set of abstractions," as Whitehead put it, sweeping every scrap of information and theory into its exclusive procedures, fixating attention and neglecting everything else in the living world.[28] Conceptual structures loom properly before us as lucid and convincing, not because they are the logical deductions of disembodied and undistracted minds, but because they are resources for enhancing, deepening, broadening and vivifying the qualitative richness and concreteness of our experience.

Growing up in the cultural greenhouses of the West, I had come a long way toward this Buddhist view of conceptual systems through a host of influences that had nothing to do with Buddhism at all, such as undergraduate courses in Bergson, Kierkegaard, William James and John Dewey, and graduate studies in Wieman, Whitehead, Hartshorne and Peirce, all of which came before a year of field work at the International Institute for Advanced Buddhistic Studies in Rangoon in 1961–1962. Buddhist involvements of the more serious kind served to italicize what I seemed always to have known—that the deepest suffering, the most transforming insight into what is fundamental and real, and the compassionate love that links people into the rhythm of life are only trivialized by conceptual form. Whatever may have been the comparative influence of Buddhism and American thinkers, it seems to me now that I have always felt that there is but one thing every child should carefully be taught to distrust. It is not the stranger but the Word, particularly the familiar Word, the one that is everywhere in the atmosphere of the society in which we are reared; the abstract summarizing Word that shrinks awareness to what is familiar and mandatory for all whose behavior would appear to make sense; the Word that makes it next to impossible to take the concrete, original feelings of a neighbor into account or even those of someone living in our own home. Buddhist and other influences persuade me that what we formulate, manipulate and control by logic and conceptual form loses in the long run its responsiveness to the vitalities of life, with the result that we experience one another inadequately and turn from the radiance that is life itself. For reasons such as these, the worst thing we ever do with words is to surrender the rich intensity and harmony of our original experience to what the definitions and sentences of a book appear to allow.

The Social Nature of Personal Identity

A fresh inquiry into the nature of human experience encounters at once the source of the fragmentation and anarchy in the contemporary world. It is the bifurcating, substantial self, the organizing principle of personal identity, the receptacle or conveyor-belt identity into which all experiences are stored, each self mutually exclusive of all others, the skin-enclosed entity whose search for identity in an ambiguous world is singled out by Ronald Laing as the great idolatry of modern youth. It is this substantial selfhood that Whitehead, according to a remark made in a seminar at

Harvard, viewed as the fundamental cause of all modern immorality in the West. A bifurcating self proliferates all the dualisms expressed in Descartes' *cogito ergo sum*—the supposititious "I" breaks up the organic unity of the world into subject and object, mind and body, man and nature, matter and spirit, time and eternity, nature and culture, which like Humpty Dumpty can never be put back together again. No cure for the linguistic bind can be expected until our attention shifts from the illusory substantial self to the living moment with all its nuclear power to link every series of events, including our own, in organic relatedness to all other centers of the living world.

In Buddhist perspectives, men and women form their identities as social facts in the course of their growth. Each momentary self freely creates a slightly new momentary self, the later one pregnant with possibilities no earlier moment could have known. Behind the vast background of feeling these novel fleeting moments *(khana-vāda)* of our lives—a background barely touched by the forms of conscious thought—like the creative energizing intuitions of life itself, which are self-corrective, self-healing and self-fulfilling. Personal identity is found in the process of aesthetic enrichment enabling us to inherit more perceptively and vividly the legacy of moments rich with quality that have been experienced in the past. The identity and order of an individual's life is either found in these passing moments— since they are all that is really real—or lost, one imperceptible drop at a time.

This is the social vision of personal identity surfacing in the writings of Hartshorne, Whitehead and Peirce. Hartshorne believes that it is chiefly a dispute about words. "The latest subject," he argues, "contains all that there is to the unity of the self as actual; the latest subject contains the whole self."[29] "My awareness of my past tends to be more vivid and direct than of the past of others, but this is no absolute difference."[30] The selfhood we attribute to ourselves, Peirce argued, "is for the most part the vulgarest delusion of vanity."[31] Whitehead contends, "The whole literature of the European races upon the subject [Personal Identity] is based upon notions which, within the last hundred years, have been completely discarded."[32] And any notion of personal identity even the most adequate one, is abstract in comparison with the concreteness of fleeting moments in the process of creative synthesis that has no end.

Buddhism has placed more emphasis than American philosophers on two features of this social perspective on personal identity. The first has to do with motivation. The greatest hunger or thirst of any person, Buddhism believes, is for direct experience of the vividness, intensity, richness and harmony of life itself. The joys of life belong to those who fight in themselves the confinements of institutional form, trusting their own original experience to acquire its compassionate forms of communication. The historical Buddha begins here the discovery that touches the core of human experience throughout the world—the awareness of original, spontaneous, personal experience, "pure experience,," as Nishida calls it, that is the source of all mankind's religions. The Buddhist symbol here is the Bodhisattva's compassion, flexible and profound in its ability to feel what moves other creatures deeply. This interrelatedness among individuals, each being the shepherd of many lives, constitutes the basis for "infinite compassion," the special legacy of Buddhism to the contemporary world. This awakened state is a higher state of vigilance than mankind thus far appears to comprehend.

The second emphasis that is distinctive of Buddhism has to do with its generalized understanding of suffering *(dukkha)*. Twenty-five centuries ago the Buddha proposed this norm for human experience: life undergoes endless suffering and degenerates when enclosed within the deadening influence and pressures of unconscious compulsive drives and habit-ridden social conformity. According to the Buddha's own teaching, such people are "writhing in delusion," suffering from trying to live against the grain, to live for the satisfaction of some overruling want or drive and thus ignore the most powerful motivation of all—the need to be faithful to the fundamental creativity of life. It was probably reflections such as these that led the Buddha to remark that "the ocean is not large and deep enough to contain the tears which through millions of existences fill the eyes of one man."[33]

In its concern with suffering, Buddhism belongs in the contemporary world as a powerful intercepter of its most self-destructive trends. Buddhism has something to say to people whose lives get caught in compulsive, conformist forms of behavior before they realize what has taken place. In its diagnosis of suffering Buddhism belongs in this world where people face the prospect of being programmed, fragmented and mobilized by a burgeoning technology with a momentum of its own. Not knowing that the resources required for curing their pathological disregard for life must be found within themselves, people seek emancipation in some of the very lifestyles that threaten the continuance of the superindustrial age. Every step taken into the higher positions of leadership removes them another unbridgeable distance from the aesthetic center of their experience. A system of habits appears to give stability and permanence to a transitory world, and they disregard all the small clues that their lives are becoming more abstract; they lose their penetrative power, and their capacity for spontaneity and fellow feeling diminishes with each passing year. There are many things about the contemporary world that remain a puzzle without a single clue, but no one need wonder what human personality, robbed of its roots in the living moment and shaped in pathological ways, should become capable of supporting cruelty beyond description, even beyond science fiction. Nuclear proliferation and the exchange of one tyranny for another are two of the few predictable features of life in the superindustrial age. Western man, in particular, has lifted himself to pinnacles of power, so high that he cannot recognize his own deepest need to be restored to the direct self-healing enjoyment of his real identity in the creativity of life.

A more reassuring feature of the social nature of personal identity is shared alike by Buddhist and now dominant trends of American philosophy. The realm of everydayness with its built-in barriers of self-centeredness, ignorance, greed, hatred and delusion is not as resistant to illumination and correction as is sometimes supposed. The deepest feelings of daily living are directly accessible to a sense of the interrelatedness of life (*pratītya-samutpāda, paticca-samuppāda* in Pali), the rich qualitative flow in the fullness of existence (*sūnyatā*) that is infinitely productive of the forms of the actual world. This perspective has been called by different names in different schools over the centuries: "conditioned genesis," "dependent origination," or, as Hajime Nakamura and Daisetz Suzuki prefer, simply "the interrelatedness of things." Each center of experience acquires its richness, not from its own self-established nature (*svabhāva*), but from feeling in our present-centeredness the feelings of fellow-creatures in a natural compassion with all that happens. One who lives in the nature of this *pratītya-samutpāda* finds that his experiences are all *sūnya* or *sūnyatā*, "emptiness not in the literal sense but in the sense of fullness of existence."[34]

Conclusion

Civilizations up to now have thwarted and destroyed the intensity and wholeness of human experience, confining feeling to insatiable wants, local, habit-ridden, parochial views, reducing life to its lowest common denominators. The few promises of breakthroughs into a larger and more generous orientation sooner or later fall under the control of the self-serving institutions of the age. No poetry, painting, nor literature with the cutting edge of tragedy in its heart seems capable of sustaining for long an awareness of the suffering and brutality that is taking place—either in the rising generations or their elders, or in any ethnic, racial, or national tradition. This is a part of the angry past that is alive in everyone today.

A new civilization without limits, however, is now beginning to assume responsibility for life on the planet; it is a civilization based for the first time in the individualized universe demanded by the aesthetic enjoyment of life, that dimension of our experience in comparison with which all else is a distraction, a delusion, a fallacy of misplaced concreteness, part of the labyrinth surrounding the independent, irreducible, substantial, fabricated, illusory selves on which "the whole literature of the European races has been based." It may be hoped that an accelerating dialogue between Buddhism and American philosophers will go far to dispel the fog that up to now has hindered individuals from coming into direct encounter with what is really real in their own experience. It may not be too much to ask, since Peirce, James, Whitehead and Hartshorne all harbor deep tendencies to reinforce, and indeed, to enlarge and clarify the perspectives that lie at the core of Buddhism, the most self-less, other-centered tradition in the history of mankind.

Prefatory Remarks to Jay McDaniel's Essay

There has been much talk of "the true self" in Zen. McDaniel uses Whiteheadian terms to tell us precisely what is meant. The true self is the present immediate act of experience; in Whitehead it is the prehensiveness that constitutes each novel form of experience. The creative act of experience unifies its actual, i.e., its past world and in this way shows the world the originality and creativity of the real, i.e., the true self. All living beings create themselves in this world-inclusive experience of the present. McDaniel uses the writings of Shin'ichi Hisamatsu to place this basic present-centeredness in the framework of a more action-oriented Zen which assumes responsibility for the social and historical world.

In ways Martin Heidegger does not concede, Buddhist meditation loosens the feelings of "mine-ness" which becloud the illumination of what is really real, leaving the future with no subjective center around which one can orient with emotional fervor and compulsiveness the life that is forever responding to life. What is real is the social process of which our own experiences are an organic part. Meditation and the enlightenment experience banish the usual conceptual overlay, enabling us to see things as they really are in their dependent origination or interrelatedness, empty of substance, full of creative immediacy, free. McDaniel shows how all of this comes to grips with the suffering and joy of the world.

Following Whitehead's invitation to look into radically different cultural worlds for "deeper meanings," McDaniel closes his essay with a discussion of what he calls "enlightened eschatology" and reminds us of Takao Tanaka's call, as a Zen thinker, for a "Buddhist natural theology" which Tanaka sees in Whitehead's thought.

4

Mahāyāna Enlightenment in Process Perspective

Jay McDaniel

In the twentieth century, several Japanese Buddhist intellectuals have suggested that in the future Mahāyāna Buddhism must become more historical in its orientation. In particular, they suggest, it must play a more active role in the development of preferred historical futures. In this context Shin'ichi Hisamatsu, a Zen Buddhist philosopher, has called for a new religious orientation in which Zen practitioners learn to understand the nature of their religion in terms of three dimensions: self, world and history. The self of which Hisamatsu speaks is what Zen Buddhists traditionally call the "true self" or "original face" of a human being. It is that arena of experience which is always here and now subjectively, but which remains unrealized until the person-centered orientation has been overcome in the enlightenment experience. In the past, says Hisamatsu, many Zen Buddhists have been active in helping others to awaken to their true selves, but they have not been active enough in helping to create alternative historical futures in which such selves, awakened or unawakened, might have better lives. If Zen activity "starts and ends only with the so-called practice of compassion involved in helping others to awaken," Hisamatsu writes, "such activity will remain unrelated to the formation of the world or creation of history, isolated from the world and history, and in the end turn Zen into a forest Buddhism, temple Buddhism, at best, a Zen monastery Buddhism"[1] Realizing that the emerging global society is one in which matters of social responsibility are as relevant as the topic of enlightenment, Hisamatsu calls for a more action-oriented Zen—one that comes out of the monastery to meet the social and historical needs of beings in the world.

The future mode of Buddhist existence envisioned by Hisamatsu can be called "enlightened eschatology." The word *eschatology* derives from the Judeao-Christian tradition where it has referred to the study of last things, that is, to the study of the coming kingdom of heaven on earth. But here the word is not used to refer to such study. Nor is it used to refer to particular doctrines involved in study of this sort. Instead, it is used to refer to the subjective way of experiencing which lies behind the formulation of such doctrines. This subjective way is one which highlights the imagining of how a society "might be" in the future, as opposed to how it "is" in the present. Of course, such imagining has been evident at various points in the history of the Mahāyāna tradition, but it has not been a dominant theme. The Mahāyāna tradition as a whole has been most noted for its enlightened attunement to the way things are, not for its eschatological consideration of how things might be. Recognizing this historical fact, Hisamatsu is calling for a new mode of Buddhist existence, one that is eschatological as well as enlightened. "Enlightened eschatology" is a convenient name for this new mode.

The purpose of this essay is to use Whiteheadian categories of thought as aids in interpreting the Mahāyāna Buddhist enlightenment experience and the way of living that results from this experience, and as aids in interpreting the phenomenological possibility of enlightened eschatology. The particular understanding of enlightenment used to represent the Mahāyāna viewpoint will be that of Zen Buddhism. The essay is divided into four sections, the first two of which define terms relevant to an interpretation of Zen enlightenment. In the first section a distinction is drawn between the "person" and the "self"—the latter term referring to what Zen Buddhists call the "true self." In the second section the way in which a true self is aware of its "person" is discussed—this awareness being what in ordinary language is called "self-consciousness," or what is better termed "person-consciousness." In the third section an interpretation of Zen enlightenment is offered using the categories of thought developed in the first two sections. And in the fourth section the phenomenological possibility of an enlightened eschatology is argued.

The Person and the Self

In order to speak of the Zen "true self" in a Whiteheadian context, this self must be distinguished from that which is denied in the traditional Buddhist doctrine of no-self *(anātman)*. Whitehead's thought and traditional

Buddhist thought are in agreement in that both deny the existence of a "substantial" self. A substantial self would be (a) an enduring substratum underlying the stream of experience constituting a person, or (b) a "subject" which stands above, behind, or apart from any particular experience as an agent or patient. To deny the existence of an underlying substratum is to suggest, conversely, that the human person is a series of fleeting, temporally discrete, causally related experiences, not an enduring substance. And to deny the existence of a substantial subject to any of these experiences is to suggest, conversely, that within each experience, there is a subjective act of experiencing the world, but no additional experiencer. Assuming this Whiteheadian and Buddhist perspective, if we analyze what appears to be a person—even if it be our own—we find nothing more than a series of experiences. The "person", as defined in this essay, is a particular series of experiences, extending from birth to physical death, taken as a whole.

The reduction of a human person into a series of experiences often yields the question: But who is it that experiences? In gazing at a wall, for example, who is gazing? In listening to a lecture, who is listening? The "who" that is sought when these questions are asked is what Zen Buddhists call the "true self." This self is not a substratum underlying the flux of experience, nor is it an entity lying behind experience as an additional experiencer. It is the experience itself, as lived from within its time of occurrence. From a Zen perspective, our true self is our immediate experience, whatever its content. If we are gazing at a wall, our self is the gazing; if we are listening to a lecture, our self is the listening; if we are reading an article, our self is the reading. In Whiteheadian terms, the true self is the present subject of experience—not as an experiencer distinct from the experiencing—but as the immediate act of experience, or the immediate act of concrescence.

In defining the self as the immediate act of experience, it is important to emphasize the temporal specification implied by the word *immediate*. To say that an act of experiencing is immediate is to say that it has subjective immediacy, or internal aliveness. In the life of a given person, it is only the present experience, not future or past experiences, that has such immediacy. Future experiences are not yet existent, and the immediacy of past experiences has already perished. It is only the present that contains the immediacy of a person's experience; therefore, it is only the present that is the self. This does not mean that the immediacy of a present experience does not perish, nor does it mean that a present experience may not be succeeded by subsequent experiences. It does mean, however, that when a present experience perishes, it ceases to be the true self of the person at issue: a new experience has become the true self of that person. Though the contents of a person's self are forever changing, since the experiences constituting that person are different at every moment, the time of the person's self is always now.

Supplementing the idea that the self of a person is always in the present, three additional points must be made about the self's nature. The first is that aspects of the entire world are immanent in the self as part of its own constitution, its own make-up. Aspects of the world form the objective data of the self's experience, and these aspects are "in" the self, not outside it. Whitehead writes, for example, that the actual world forms the "objective content" of immediate experience: "The world within experience is identical with the world beyond experience, the occasion of experience is within the world and the world is within the occasion."[2] And Zen Buddhists write: "mountains and rivers, the earth, grass and trees, tiles and stones, all of these are the self's original part."[3] The point made here is that a human being's self, by its very nature, is open to and inclusive of the experienced world. A self is not an isolated mind or a subjective container closed off from an external world. It is an open field of awareness within which the world lies and through which the world is unified from a particular spatio-temporal perspective. In this context it is noteworthy that the object of much Buddhist meditative practice is to eliminate from this field of awareness certain intellectual and emotional prejudices which habitually plague it, so that the objective world can be perceived with greater clarity and appreciation. In seeing the world this way, a person is seeing the very content of his or her own true self. As the self's objective content, the world *is* the self.

The second point to be noted about the self is that it is, or can be, creative in the way it includes the world. The historical records of Zen Buddhism are replete with stories of monks and masters who demonstrate their true selves, not by passively gazing at walls, but by creating, in word and deed, novel responses to given situations. For example, a monk might ask a Zen master about the location of the true self, and the master might respond by stepping on the monk's foot. In part, the master's behavior is meant to provoke his cohort into realizing that his (the monk's) true self is standing in the present, asking the question; and in part, the master's response is a way in which he shows the monk the originality and creativity of his (the master's) own true self. To an observer, the master's response may seem irrational. From the master's perspective, however, his behavior is authentically religious because authentic religion should, by definition, involve originality.

Philosophically, the importance of originality in Mahāyāna Buddhism is generalized by the contemporary Zen philosopher Keiji Nishitani in his insistence that, in their innermost selves, all living beings are self-creative. They "are in attainment of themselves" at every moment; they "posit themselves, affirm themselves"; they are acts of "be-ification."[4] Nishitani explains that the outward form and behavior of a living being is an expression of its inner subjective creativity, its inner true self. The originality of a Zen master is simply a particular instance of a more general principle found throughout the world of nature. Analogously, Whitehead speaks of the subjective reality of a living being, human or nonhuman, as involving self-creativity whereby the being at issue creates its own determination form for others to experience. Like a Zen true self, a Whiteheadian occasion of experience, viewed from within its own perspective, is passive in its openness to the world and yet active in its own self-creativity. Self-creativity and openness do not exclude one another; they are two aspects of the same immediate self.

The third point to be noted about the self is that it is inherently finite. Following Heidegger, it might be said that the self is being-towards-death; though it is more appropriate to say that the self *is* a death. As a Zen thinker puts it: "Once we have taken life subjectively we realize that life and death are not two separate things. We do not find ourselves moving from life to death, but living and at the same time dying."[5] This is Whitehead's perpetual perishing, viewed from the inside. From this perspective perishing is not something the self observes as a datum; it is something the self *is* in its innermost identity. At each moment that the self experiences its world and gathers it into unity, it dies into the world it experiences. In human life there seems to be no alternative to this fact; to be a self and to be temporally finite are two sides of one coin.

To summarize what has been said thus far, the distinction between the self and the person should be reiterated. The "self" is that finite, self-creative, world-inclusive experience which, for a given individual, occurs in the present. The "person" is the series of finite, self-creative, world inclusive experiences which, when they are in the immediacy of occurring, are "selves." When an experience constituting the life of a person is in the past or future, that is, when it is not in the process of occurring, it is not the person's "self." The self is always in the present, never in the past or future. The self is the subjective space in which a person's immediacy, whatever its content, resides.

Person-Consciousness

The subjective immediacy of a person's self is never an object for itself. This is to say, in Whiteheadian terms, that the prehensions constituting an act of concrescence are not objects, or data, for the act at issue. They are acts of experiencing, but they are not items experienced. Thus, if a person is perceiving a tree, the immediacy of that person's self is the act of perceiving, but it is not the tree that is perceived, nor is it an object standing alongside the tree. Similarly, if a person is remembering a past experience, then the self is an act of remembering, but it is not the experience remembered. In its immediacy the self is not a thing among things, or a datum among data. It does not know itself in the same way it knows the data it experiences. This raises the question of how experiences of "self-consciousness" can be interpreted.

Traditional Western philosophy offers at least two models in terms of which self-conscious experience might be understood: one is represented by Descartes, the other by Kant and the German idealists.[6] In the *Meditations* Descartes suggests that self-consciousness is a matter of direct self-reflexivity. A thinking "I" turns in upon itself in order to become aware of itself without reference to the world or to the body. In the Kantian tradition, on the other hand, it is suggested that self-consciousness is a matter of indirect or mediated reflexivity. A self knows itself in being aware of a world other than itself; hence, self-consciousness is mediated by a consciousness of the world. From the point of view of this essay, there is much to be said for the Kantian tradition. There would be no subjective experience to reflect upon without a world which is subjectively experienced. But there exists a problem with both the Kantian and the Cartesian models if, in articulating them, the word *reflexivity* is used, for it inevitably implies the existence of a substantial subject which can turn toward itself, even if only in an indirect manner. Just as the Cartesian notion of unmediated reflexivity implies the notion of a subject which turns toward itself without reference to the world, so the Kantian tradition can imply the notion of a subject which turns toward itself through reference to the world. The view of this essay is that the subject is the subjectivity. It cannot turn toward itself, or prehend itself. It can only turn toward the world. This means that given traditional connotations of the phrase "self-consciousness," the self is inherently un-self-conscious.

To say that the self is inherently un-self-conscious is to say, as was said above, that the immediacy of the self is not a datum for itself. The self is never conscious "of" its immediacy. This does not mean, however, that the self lacks internal aliveness. The self has within its act of experiencing a kind of enjoyment whereby it has intrinsic value for itself. In this enjoyment there is no distinction between subject and object, or between what is enjoyed and the act of enjoying. The enjoyment is the immediacy of the act of experiencing, with no "I" for whom the immediacy is immediate.

Though the enjoyment inherent in immediate experience is the locus of lived value for any living being, this enjoyment is not necessarily "personal." The subjectivity of a cellular event, for example, is an act of enjoying, as is that of any living non-human organism, but these modes of subjective enjoyment need not have a "personal" quality. It is doubtful, for example, that a living cell experiences itself as a human person among persons. Furthermore, much human experience is enjoyable without being personal. The subjectivity of an experience in deep sleep may be enjoyable, but not especially personal, as may that of a spontaneous moment of self-forget-fulness. That which makes experience personal, from the point of view of this essay, is what is normally called "self-consciousness"; and that to which the phrase "self-consciousness" ought to refer is better termed "person-consciousness." It is when immediate experience becomes person-conscious that it becomes personal.

Person-consciousness occurs when a self becomes conscious of past and future experiences within the particular psychic stream to which it belongs. The experience in this psychic stream are part of the self's person, and the explicit awareness of these experiences is the self's consciousness of its person, or its person-consciousness. From an external perspective the self is one among many experiences in the life of its person. From an internal perspective, however, the person is a cluster of anticipated and remembered data available to be experienced, in a positive or negative way, by the self. When a man remembers an experience from early childhood, for example, his immediate self is prehending an experience in the life of his person, and he has become person-conscious. And when a woman anticipates an experience in the future, her self is prehending an aspect of her future person as a possibility for subsequent actualization, and she has become person-conscious. Whereas the external perspective gives priority to the person as a point of departure for understanding the self, the internal perspective gives priority to the self as a point of departure for understanding the person. In understanding person-consciousness, the internal perspective is preferable because it accentuates the fact that the existential point of departure for person-consciousness is in fact immediate experience as lived in the present.

When immediate experience, or the immediate self, is conscious of its person, it is conscious of a cluster of data in its world. In this particular instance, the world is not the physical world perceived through the senses; it is an internal world perceived through memory and anticipation. But the difference between this internal world and the physical world is one of quality, not of metaphysical principle. In principle, the physical world perceived through sense-perception and the internal world perceived through memory and anticipation are part of one world—the world given for perception in immediate experience. When a self turns toward its past or future person, it is simply turning toward a particular type of datum in its overall world. One objective of Buddhist meditation, as will be explained in the following section, is to disengage the self, at least for a brief moment, from attachment to its person, so that it can become more open to the rest of its world.

Enlightenment

In a Mahāyāna context, the word *enlightenment* has two referents. It refers to an enlightenment experience, and it refers to an enlightened way of experiencing that succeeds the experience. Many non-Buddhists conceive enlightenment only in the first sense as an experience to be gradually attained or suddenly acquired with disciplined meditational effort and insight. But the dominant traditions within Mahāyāna Buddhism stress that the experience itself is only the beginning of enlightenment proper, the latter being a subjective way that informs everyday life. To cling to the enlightenment experience at the expense of the way of experiencing is to be unenlightened. In discussing enlightenment as a whole, then, it is necessary to interpret both the experience and the way of experiencing, remembering that the latter is the most important. Though Buddhists often avoid the language of means and end, it might be appropriate to say that the enlightenment experience, rather than being an end in itself, is a means toward the enlightened way of experiencing. The way itself is the end. When one lives this way, there is then no other end to seek.

The Enlightenment Experience. The enlightenment experience in Zen Buddhism has at least two sides: a negative side in which certain types of personal experience are cut off, and a positive side in which a new psychological and ontological perspective is acquired.

The Negative Side. The negative side of the enlightenment experience is what Zen Buddhists traditionally call the "great death" of an ego-centered orientation. In a Whiteheadian context this death can be interpreted as the cutting off of certain forms of personal experience and their existential undercurrents in meditation. The forms of personal experience eliminated in great death fall into three categories, to be summarized at the end of the following discussion.

First, all conscious and reflective feelings of the personal past and future are eliminated in the great death. These feelings are specific components of what Whitehead calls the "mental pole" of present experience. They are acts of thinking about "who I was" in the past or "who I will be" in the future. The "I" itself is a cognitive object projected by such feelings, often representing the active side of actual or potential experiences. (The "me"—as a direct object—would be a similar object, often representing the passive side of such experiences.) In Zen meditation these acts of thinking are eliminated through sustained concentration on a psychological object such as a kōan. Complete concentration on the object over a long period of time results in the dissolution of all intellectual feelings, including those that are person-conscious. As a consequence, there exists in the mind of the meditator a state of pure alertness in which there is no thought of an "I" or "me" being alert. Moments of extreme concentration in ordinary life—for example, when one is absorbed in an immediate task— may approximate this kind of experience. In such cases all conscious feelings constituting person-consciousness are eliminated, while the self is persistently absorbed in its attention to an immediate datum of experience.

The elimination of person-consciousness in the enlightened experience is not, however, the only kind of psychic elimination required for the great death. If this were so, individuals who had moments of extreme concentration would have undergone the equivalent of a Zen great death, in which case their subjective mode of experiencing would be on a qualitative par with that of the enlightened Buddhist. Observation suggests that people who have moments of great concentration are not necessarily enlightened, and hence that other aspects of personal experience must be eliminated in the great death—aspects which are not eliminated in mundane moments of concentration. Among these aspects are certain subconscious feelings which ordinarily link a person's self with her or his personal past, even when the self is not explicitly person-conscious.

From a Whiteheadian perspective, there are two types of subconscious feeling which might cause a self to be subconsciously influenced by its personal past, and which might be candidates for elimination in the Zen great death: pure physical feelings and hybrid feelings.[7] For the most part, when Whitehead speaks of perception in the mode of casual efficacy, he is speaking of pure physical feelings. These are feelings in which physical experiences belonging to the past are subconsciously remembered and preserved in the present. From Whitehead's point of view, it is metaphysically necessary, if there is to be any continuity between past and present, that each experience in the life of a living being begin with pure physical feelings of its past physical experiences. Consequently, if it is assumed, as it should be, that a Zen practitioner maintains some sort of continuity between his present and his past amidst meditation, then it can also be assumed that simple physical feelings of the past are not eliminated in meditation. Even if the Zen meditator begins to lose attachment to his past person, he remains a part of the particular psychic stream, or the particular person, to which he is becoming unattached.

Hybrid feelings, however, do provide a proper candidate for elimination in the great death. These are acts of experiencing in which mental experiences belonging to the personal past are remembered in the present in a subconscious way. The data of such remembering would be thoughts, feeling-tones, and images from a person's past intellectual life—items which surface, for example, in dreams and other semiconscious states. In arguing for hybrid feelings as candidates for elimination in the great death, three points need to be made. The first is simply that hybrid feelings can in fact be eliminated, because they are not necessary for the occurrence of experience in living beings. The second point to note is that the practice of Zen does seem to involve the elimination of data analogous to those eliminated if hybrid feelings were to cease. In Zen, for example, when dream-like images from the personal past emerge in meditative states, these data are considered as obstacles to the attainment of post-personal experience, rather than as aids in personal growth. The master urges the practitioner to ignore them and to continue concentration until the images gradually subside. From a Whiteheadian perspective, the dissolution of such data would logically result from the elimination of hybrid feelings.

The third reason for choosing hybrid feelings as likely candidates for elimination in the Zen great death pertains to the role hybrid feelings normally play in an individual's subconscious sense of personal identity. As Whitehead suggests and as John Cobb has elaborated, hybrid prehensions, while not metaphysically necessary for experience to occur, are in fact necessary if the present self is to be identified with its personal past in a distinctive way.[8] In this cosmic epoch, suggests Whitehead, pure physical feelings remember only those experiences in the past, including the personal past, which are immediately contiguous in time and space. This means that, with pure physical feeling alone, a present self might experience an identity with its personal past of seconds prior, but that any sense of identity with experiences of days, months, and years prior would be obviated by a sense of greater identity with immediately contiguous influences stemming from the body. With hybrid prehensions, however, the limitations of spatial and temporal contiguity are lifted. Whitehead suggests that hybrid prehensions can feel the noncontiguous personal past in a direct and unmediated manner, and Cobb shows that it is just such subconscious remembering that establishes the distinctive sense of personal identity over time which human beings ordinarily experience.

For many in the West, the sense of personal identity of which Cobb speaks is doubtless considered an essential prerequisite to meaningful existence. From the Buddhist point of view, however, this sense of identity can also be considered as a way in which a present self is subconsciously enslaved to its past. In Buddhist terms, the mentality of the personal past that is carried along through subconscious memories can be one form of personal "karma"—a karma that needs to be transcended, at least for a moment. The object of Buddhist meditation is the cutting off of the karma so that the self can be liberated for a new mode of existence. In Whiteheadian terms it can thus be suggested that karma—as the direct subconscious influence of the non-contiguous personal past—is eliminated in meditation through the elimination of hybrid feelings, even as the fact of personal identity with the past is maintained in the experience of the Zen practitioner through pure physical feelings. As with the elimination of conscious feelings constituting person-consciousness, the elimination of subconscious hybrid feelings or karma occurs through intense concentration on, and absorption in, a non-personal datum such as bodily breathing or a kōan. As absorption in the datum increases, hybrid feelings gradually subside until, at one crucial point, the direct subconscious link with the mentality of the personal past is cut off. Past thoughts and attitudes then cease to have their subconscious hold on the present self, or, in Buddhist terms, the bonds of karma have been broken. Immediately after this psychic death, hybrid prehensions can and do re-emerge, as is evidenced by the fact that enlightened Buddhists who have undergone the great death subsequently remember their personal pasts in an immediate way. But even as hybrid feelings re-emerge, the true self of the enlightened Buddhist has been liberated from habitual bondage to the past. The breaking of the bonds of karma in the great death initiates a new way of experiencing, one that is grounded in the immediate present rather than in memories of the past.

Besides feelings of person-consciousness and subconscius hybrid feelings, however, a third aspect of personal experience must be negated in the great death if the way of experiencing that follows thereafter is to be fully understood. This aspect of experience is not a type of feeling but a way of feeling or a subjective form. In particular, it is a subjective form which often accompanies anticipatory feelings of future personal possibilities. It is what Buddhists traditionally call "attachment to the ego," or what can here be called "the subjective form of mine-ness."

The word "mine-ness" is an English translation of Heidegger's term *Jemeinigkeit,* which refers to a quality of experience characteristic of the way a human being anticipates his or her personal possibilities. Through the subjective form of mine-ness as interpreted by Heidegger and in this essay, future personal possibilities are felt as "mine"—that is, as centers of subjective emphasis in terms of which life has meaning and in terms of which the rest of the world is perceived. When the quality of mine-ness pervades anticipatory person-consciousness, items in the experienced world are perceived in light of the fact that they are useful for the enhancement of anticipated personal possibilities, with the possibilities being primary points of emotional reference. This mode of perception and this type of emphasis are no doubt central in much ordinary experience. Whereas Heidegger's analysis of human nature might suggest that the quality of mine-ness is an incorrigible adjunct of anticipatory person-consciousness, Buddhist experience, however, suggests that mine-ness need not dominate human experience, and that the elimination of mine-ness can in fact enhance the quality of such experience.

Consider, for example, two selves. One self might anticipate its possibilities with a relative degree of impartiality so that items in its world are felt as intrinsic realities for themselves, whereas another self might anticipate its possibilities with a subjective attachment that precludes such appreciation. The first self anticipates with a low degree of mine-ness, and the second with a high degree of mine-ness. From a Buddhist perspective, the first self mentioned above has attained a mode of subjective enjoyment that is rich with inner beauty and subjective form—a mode centered in the immediacy of the present rather than in the personal future. The absence of mine-ness as a particular subjective form allows for the presence of other subjective forms which are both sympathetic to the immediate environment and emotionally satisfying to the immediate self. The second self, however, has lost sight of the value of items in its environment and misses the enjoyment of the immediate present, because it over-emphasizes the importance of future personal possibilities. The final objective of

Buddhist meditation is not the elimination of reflective person-consciousness or the elimination of hybrid feelings, but rather the elimination of that subjective attachment, the subjective form of "mine-ness", which often accompanies anticipatory person-consciousness. Concomitant with the elimination of all reflective feelings in the great death comes the elimination of anticipatory person consciousness, which in turn results in the elimination of mine-ness. Following this death, anticipatory person-consciousness re-emerges, though without the subjective form of mine-ness. The enlightened Buddhist can then anticipate his or her personal future, but this future is no longer the subjective center around which life is oriented. The immediate self has become that center.

In summary, the great death of the Zen enlightenment experience involves the cutting off, for a brief moment, of three aspects of personal experience. It involves the cessation of ordinary feelings of person-consciousness; the elimination of subconscious hybrid feelings of the personal past; and the dissolution of the subjective form of mine-ness. The cutting off of such feelings is not an end in itself, but a means toward the acquisition of a new mode of experiencing which results from a new psychological point of view and fresh ontological insights that emerge in the enlightenment experience. This new point of view and these insights form the positive side of the experience.

The Positive Side. The positive side of the enlightenment experience is grounded in the realization that the immediacy of experience, or the self, is distinct from the person to which it was formerly bound. The self is able to see the world from its own immediate perspective, and it is able to see that the person to which it was once attached is but one of many items in its own psychological world. Having eliminated the bonds of karma and attachment to the ego, the self becomes aware of its own radical freedom. It is free from the habit and repetition which previously derived from subconscious links with its person, and it is free for an immediate creativity in the present. Thus the Zen master will confirm the enlightenment of his student, not when the student reflects upon the enlightenment experience and says "I am enlightened," but rather when the student spontaneously expresses his or her freedom by demonstrating it creatively.

The ontological insight that accompanies the new psychological point of view is first of all an understanding of the above-mentioned freedom. In Whiteheadian terms, it is realized that the metaphysical ultimate is Creativity rather than a creator God; or, in Zen terms, it is realized that the ultimate is a subjective Emptiness. A definition of the word *Emptiness* is in order here. While the word has been used in different contexts in the history of Buddhism, it is used by contemporary Japanese Buddhist thinkers such as Shin'ichi Hisamatsu to denote an ultimate that has its actuality, not apart from immediate experience, but in the creativity of such experience. Analogously, the Whiteheadian ultimate, Creativity, is an ultimate that is actual in virtue of its subjective exemplifications, rather than apart from them. An understanding of Emptiness as thus defined or of Whitehead's Creativity involves, then, a realization that the subjective immediacy of experience is something created by itself rather than by God. The ultimate metaphysical fact is not that God creates the immediacy of the self, but that the self creates its own immediacy. From a Whiteheadian perspective this does not mean that there is no God. It does mean, however, that the self of God is but one among many instances of subjective self-creativity, rather than the sole instance. It also means that God, while an important factor in the universe, is not the metaphysical ultimate. Creativity, or Emptiness, is that which is ultimate.

The feeling of creativity that arises in the enlightenment experience is not, however, a feeling of being isolated from the world, but a feeling of being "with" the world and this for two reasons. In the first place, it is realized with vividness that the world outside experience is identical with the world within experience, or, to say the same thing, that the actual world is the objective content of experience. This does not mean that the self produces the content of the physically experienced world; it means that the physically experienced world produces the content of the self, even as the self creates its own immediacy. This is the traditional Buddhist doctrine of dependent origination viewed from the inside. A person's self, even as self-creative, is an act of experiencing the world and gathering it into subjective unity. In doing this, the self is dependent on the world it experiences. It "originates in dependence" on this world.

In the second place, the feeling of being a self-creative self is one of being "with" the world, because in the enlightenment experience, a certain mode of perception is uncovered whereby the self can feel the subjectivity of other beings directly. This mode of perception is what Whitehead calls perception in the mode of casual efficacy. It consists of feelings which *feel the feelings* of other actual beings conformally. Whitehead suggests that this mode of perception is the ground of all experience, and thus that the primitive mode of human experience is a natural and unobstructed sympathy with all that is actual. In ridding experience of its usual conceptual overlay through the enlightenment experience, Buddhists recover this mode of perception and thus become directly aware in an intuitive manner of the subjective side of an allegedly "objective' world. Following the enlightenment experience, Buddhists recur to normal modes of perception (Whitehead's "symbolic reference"), but they are attuned in a unique way to that side of the symbolically perceived world which is causally objectified through its feeling tones, as distinct from that side which is presentationally objectified. To be attuned to the subjective side of the perceived world in this way is, from a Buddhist perspective, to see things as they really are. On the one hand, such seeing involves the perception of events in the world as instances of dependent origination; things are no-things because they arise in dependence on other things. On the other hand, such seeing involves the perception of no-things as actualities with intrinsic value for themselves. That beings are empty of substance means that they are full of immediacy and creativity and empty of substance. The enlightenment experience awakens the self to this "fullness of what is empty" and "emptiness of what is full."

The Enlightened Way of Experiencing. The enlightened way of experiencing grows naturally out of the new psychological perspective and new ontological insights acquired in the enlightenment experience. In Zen this way of experiencing involves a radical freedom from moment to moment in the life of a person, with each moment realizing itself as a self discontinuous from the psychic past and future because the bonds of karma have been cut off. It also involves a wisdom in which the physically felt world is approached as being empty of substance yet full of subjectivity, and a compassion in which the self spontaneously identifies with the subjectivity of what is felt. The life of freedom, wisdom, and compassion is the enlightened way, directly expressive of the way things are. The fact that the enlightened way expresses the way things are is its inherent truthfulness.

As Whitehead well recognized, however, it is not simply the truthfulness of a way of experiencing that gives it value. In itself a truthfulness relation to the experienced world is valuable only insofar as it serves the enjoyment of qualitative beauty in experience. "Beauty is left as the one aim which by its nature is self-justifying."[9] The quality of enjoyment or beauty in the enlightened way is what gives it its final self-justification. This quality pertains more to the emotional tenor of the way than to its cognitive implications. In Zen this emotional tenor is represented by the expression: "Every day is a good day." This expression does not refer to the state of the objective world experienced. Zen Buddhists, like most human beings, are aware of objective conditions in the world which could be improved.

Instead the saying refers to *how* the objective world is felt from within, that is, to the character of the subjective form of enlightened experiencing. As the stories of Zen masters suggest, subjective forms such as pain, pleasure, anger, joy, and sorrow are part and parcel of the enlightened way. Zen masters are sorrowful at the death of loved ones; angry when their students are lazy; happy when their students show progress; and they experience physical pain on the occurrence of bodily injury. Contrary to Whitehead's own understanding of Buddhism, the enlightened way is not anesthetic. It does not block out the world experienced, but feels it through normal human emotions, and it is such emotions that make life worth living.

What the enlightened way does lack, however, is a particular emotion: the subjective form of mine-ness. The attachment to personal possibilities whereby the world becomes an object of manipulation is minimized in the life that follows the enlightenment experience. This does not mean that the enlightened self does not have person-conscious feelings. Following the enlightenment experience, Buddhists are aware of their own psychic pasts, and they anticipate future personal possibilities, as do other human beings. But the subjective forms qualifying such anticipatory feelings are mine-less rather than mine-full. Future possibilities are not felt as centers in terms of which the experienced world is evaluated; they are experienced as a cluster of possibilities among many—a cluster which may or may not be relevant to the immediate situation. The intrinsic enjoyment of experience is thus divorced from a person-centered orientation, and the harmony and intensity of experience is enhanced. The immediate self is more open to its world and thus experiences it more harmoniously than before; it is open to possibilities for creativity inherent in the moment and thus experience more intensely than before. In this context the immediate self can and often does anticipate its personal future, but in such cases the center of enjoyment is in the immediate activity of anticipating, not in the objective possibility anticipated. Even when the self aims at its personal tomorrow, the salvation of the self is today.

Enlightened Eschatology

The interpretation of enlightenment offered above provides a theoretical basis for showing the phenomenological possibility for an enlightened way of experiencing being, which is at the same time, an eschatological way. One mode of existence is "phenomenologically" compatible with another if the first involves types of feelings and subjective forms which can be included in the second. The enlightened mode of experiencing precludes no particular types of feelings or subjective forms, except the subjective form of mine-ness. If an eschatological mode of existence involves feelings and subjective forms which can themselves preclude the subjective form of mine-ness, then an enlightened mode can be eschatological.

An eschatological mode of existence oriented toward action in history involves at least three types of feelings and one subjective form. In the first place it involves imaginative feelings which prehend possibilities distinct from those actualized in the social and historical present. Secondly, it involves anticipatory feelings which prehend a future as predicated of these novel possibilities. Third, it involves person-conscious feelings which anticipate future personal action aimed at contributing to the actualization of the novel historical future. And fourth, it involves a subjective form, not of resignation or despair, but of hope. Without the imagination of novel possibilities, an anticipated historical future would be identical to that of the present or past. Without anticipation of the future, the imagination would only be anticipating possibilities for the immediate present. Without person-consciousness committed to future personal action, the imagination and anticipation of novel historical futures would be mere daydreams. And without the hope that an anticipated future can actually come into existence, there would be no motive for an imaginative anticipation of future personal action. Taken together, then, these three types of feelings and this particular subjective form are the phenomenological constituents of the eschatological orientation. They are what is involved when a social prophet, whether Jesus or Marx, imagines a new kind of future for the world; and they are what must be involved if Zen Buddhism is to become, as Hisamatsu suggests, "world forming and history creating."[10]

In the eschatological traditions of the West—prophetic Judaism, prophetic Christianity, and Marxism among them—a person-centered approach to the eschatological future has no doubt been predominant. The kind of ego-attachment which the Mahāyāna way transcends has been integral to the restlessness which pervades much of Western experience. This means that much Western experience has involved, not only the imaginative and active anticipation of alternative historical futures, but the anticipation of such futures with an emphasis that places future personal gratification at the center of subjective concern. Such emphasis is the subjective form of mine-ness. But there is no reason in principle why an enlightened self might not anticipate the same sorts of futures without this subjective form. Feelings belonging to the eschatological way do not necessitate a subjective form of mine-ness; and the enlightened way does not preclude such feelings. Thus an enlightened eschatology is a phenomenological possibility. In fact, it is a phenomenological "actuality" as evidenced in Hisamatsu's own call for a new kind of Buddhism. In calling for a Buddhism that is "world forming and history creating," Hisamatsu is himself imagining a novel possibility, predicating it of an historical future, and hoping that it will come into existence. The focus of this point is not on the state of affairs for which Hisamatsu calls, but on the feelings exemplified in his act of calling. They are precisely those feelings which are present in the eschatological orientation. Presuming that Hisamatsu is enlightened amid his actualization of these types of feelings, his enlightened mode of existence is, at the same time, an eschatological mode. His anticipation of a novel future for Zen Buddhists and his activity of aiming toward that future are thus examples of enlightened eschatology, the very phenomenon for which he calls.

In principle, an enlightened eschatology could involve the integration of self-interest and altruism in a unique way. If, as this essay suggests, the enlightened way involves enjoying the here and now of experiencing in a manner that is divorced from attachment (but not attention) to personal possibilities, then in the enlightened way the imaginative experiencing of alternative futures is immediately enjoyable in the present, even as it aims to enhance the welfare of others. This enjoyment in the present is a form of "self-interest," given the meaning of the term "self" employed in this essay; the aim to help others might be called "altruism"; and thus the enjoyment amidst such aiming would be altruistic self-interest, or "self-enjoying" altruism. The self, of course, is not an object enjoyed; it is the immediacy of enjoying. What is enjoyed in a self-enjoying altruism is the very act of aiming to help others.

If enlightened eschatology and self-enjoying altruism are to become a real alternative for Buddhism in the future, however, a philosophical framework congenial to their development must be articulated. A given way of experiencing is most consistently actualized when its actualizers hold views which render the way intelligible given the nature of things. If, for example, an existential perspective is articulated in doctrines that assert the primacy of a substantial self, the enlightened way of experiencing will appear unintelligible and counter to the nature of things. Or if an existential perspective is articulated in doctrines that deny the distinction between an already determined past and a possible future, an eschatological way of experiencing will appear counter to the nature of things. In itself, a way of experiencing is more than a way of thinking about the world and thinking is simply one form of feeling. Nevertheless, clarity of thought can itself enhance the development of authentic ways of experiencing.

One possibility for Buddhist philosophers in the future might lie in an appropriation of Whitehead's philosophy as a vehicle for articulating their own views of what Buddhism can and ought to be in the future. The categories of Whitehead's thought might show how an enlightened eschatology can express, rather than contradict, the very nature of things. In this regard it is worthy of note that a Zen Buddhist thinker in Japan has already suggested that a "Buddhist natural theology" based on Whitehead's thought is both possible and desirable.[11] Needless to say, the development of such a theology would uncover many aspects of Whitehead's thought congenial to the traditional Zen point of view, and other aspects which diverge from traditional Zen emphases. The resulting theology would be in effect neo-Buddhist—a Buddhist process theology.

Whether Buddhists do or do not find Whitehead's thought useful in articulating their own perspectives, however, Whitehead's thought might be useful to those philosophers in the West or East who seek philosophical dialog with Buddhist traditions. One issue with which these thinkers might deal could be enlightenment itself, in which case the line of thought outlined in the first three sections of this essay might prove useful. Another issue might be the relation between enlightenment and social ethics, in which case the notion of enlightened eschatology discussed in brief in this section might be further developed. The development of philosophy of enlightened eschatology could be a task for cross-cultural philosophers who seek to go beyond the stage of comparing and contrasting Eastern and Western thought forms toward the integration of aspects of each into novel philosophical wholes. Whitehead himself challenged thinkers in the East and West to begin "looking to each other for deeper meanings."[12] This essay has attempted to show how aspects of his thought might be useful in responding to that challenge.

Prefatory Remarks to Kenneth Inada's Essay

*One of the leading philosophers in Buddhistic Studies in the United States
addresses here a specific question: At what point is the Buddhist encounter
with American thought most far-reaching and profound? At what point is
the encounter mutually reinforcing and capable of generating a new transparency with regard to what is deepest in the American experience? With
scholarship in Buddhism being systematically upgraded, and with English
becoming the universal vehicle of Buddhist thought, answers will not be long
in coming. Midway in the present century, investigations of Buddhism became
more serious, lost the atmosphere of faddishness, freed themselves from damaging
misconceptions stemming from Schopenhauer, emerged from European tendencies
to see Buddhism as a mere extension of Hinduism, and with academic
interchange accelerating between Asia and the West, reached a position where
it is now capable of asking the truly generic Buddhist questions. Without
falling into the mysticism that usually follows such questions in the West,
Buddhism wonders about the naivety of the way the long tradition of
empiricism in Anglo-American philosophy takes as its point of departure a
subject that perceives the objects of the world and thus leaves the bifurcating
mind a mystery in the very reality it seeks to understand. From a Buddhist
point of view, neither the knower nor the one-sided, culture-bound knowledge
is really natural, strictly speaking, to the nature of things. The doctrine of
śūnyatā penetrates to the core of all experiences, more than mere emptiness
or receptacle or vacuity, as is sometimes asserted. Śūnyatā is that which
makes the process of relational origination or conditioned genesis possible; it
is the source of the depth and profundity of the arts and sciences of civilization.
What are the chances now for an American involvement with śūnyatā?
"Excellent," Inada replies, and tells us why.*

5

The American Involvement with Śūnyatā: Prospects

Kenneth K. Inada

Historically, Buddhism was the last of the great Asiatic schools of thought to reach the American shores. Yet, today, it has become the strongest and most influential force from Asia to grace the four corners of America. From intellectual understanding to meditational practices at Zen Centers, for example, Americans are readily accepting some elements of its philosophy as viable supplements to their ways of life.

The question that immediately arises is: Do Americans really understand Buddhism in its fullest dimensions? Or is their attraction more faddish and superficial than serious and profound? Have they had available to them the major Buddhist perspectives in terms they could understand?

The answers to these questions are admittedly unclear, indecisive, and complex. It is true that Buddhism entered America quietly without much fanfare. It is also true that it entered without a systematic program of propagation by any group. It probably arrived first with the Asian immigrants as part of their cultural traditions but it also came to the American intellectuals via Europe. In the beginning, only a small percentage of the intelligentsia was exposed to Buddhism, and most of them came out of curiosity and very few with any seriousness to engage themselves in the Asian cultural dynamics. Distortions and indeed misconceptions of Buddhist principles have been a prominent part of the Buddhist pageant in both Europe and the United States.

From the beginning, Europe entertained Buddhism under the larger religious rubric of Indian religion which was mainly Hinduism. Of course, this was not entirely the fault of Europeans since native Indians themselves had a natural tendency to foster such an identity, treating Buddhism as nothing but an extension of Hinduism. Contemporary Indians by and large still return to and nestle in this basic misunderstanding. Some of the doctrines used in Hinduism, but modified drastically by Buddhism, still retain a Hinduistic flavor and character. The venerable Sarvepalli Radhakrishnan, for example, made such a great impact on the West with his monumental two-volume work, *Indian Philosophy,*[1] in which he persuasively expounded the fundamentally Hinduistic approach to Buddhism, that the Western mind could not completely disengage itself from this erroneous or misleading image of Buddhism. Under its shadow, misconceptions were further generated and perpetuated. Buddhism became tainted and relegated to a restricted form of religion and philosophy. Such being the case, there was little room for its development and growth.

One of the most damaging misconceptions was the label of Buddhist pessimism. For example, Arthur Schopenhauer had concluded rather hastily that the Buddhist pessimistic philosophy was a fact and thereafter his views were uncritically accepted and carried through to the 20th century. And so we note such formidable men as R. W. Emerson, J. Royce and A. N. Whitehead perpetuating, consciously or unconsciously, the pessimistic view of life. In short, Buddhism was either denied exposure to its true value or used as a vehicle to transport and support the thinker's own viewpoints or doctrines.

This is indeed a naive understanding, but it also depicts a rather dismal situation. In a way, the pessimistic spirit only prolonged the alienation and distraction of Buddhism. It prevented American thinkers from seriously engaging themselves in the full challenge of Buddhist principles. Josiah Royce, for example, lacked the basic understanding for the Buddhist interpretational challenge. His approach was idealistic in the large scheme of things but his treatment of Buddhist principles was indeed narrow; that is to say, they were never really digested and incorporated into his system. They stood aside or apart and were only beckoned at convenient moments to ensure the establishment of his grand idealistic thought system. Furthermore, he was confused about the Hindu and Buddhist framework and ignorant of the attendant differences between the two. Even the redoubtable Whitehead was remiss in his understanding of Buddhist spirit and principles. It is one of the ironies of our times that despite his conscious rejection of Buddhism, his own philosophy came very close to it. Over in Europe curiously enough, men like Heidegger, Buber, Jaspers, certain existentialists and theologians developed their systems somewhat by the direct or indirect influence of Buddhism.

At any rate, the first half of our century has been a time of exposure to Asiatic thought, with Buddhism leading the way. Yet, up to the mid-century, there has been no well planned, systematic studies of Buddhist principles. Much of Buddhist thought was fragmentarily, cursorily and even popularly disseminated. The postwar beat generation in a way contributes to the serious engagement with Asiatic philosophies, especially Zen. The mid-century, however, is a good convenient mark to herald a new start, a new beginning, in the serious academic, intellectual and practical approach to Buddhism.[2] Roughly since then, a new crop of American scholars have appeared who are well trained in the languages of Buddhism, some with practical experiences in Asia proper, and also well trained in the methodology and disciplines of the West. These young scholars are already making headway in Buddhistic studies in all areas. Moreover, Buddhist scholars from the Asiatic countries have come to America in increasing numbers and some have taken up permanent residence. Similarly, European scholars have crossed the Atlantic and are making significant contributions in the Buddhist scene. At the same time, the spirit of Buddhism is being fired to new heights by the continuous presence of Asiatic religionist leaders who bring their Buddhist wares directly into the American experience by establishing centers of meditational practice. On the whole, they have been very successful. And finally, most American institutions of higher learning have now established some form of Asian Studies which include Buddhist thought and culture. Thus on a broad front, Buddhism is being exposed to the Americans in rather strong doses.[3]

In consequence, we are now witnessing in America the most auspicious concentration of Buddhist studies and practice ever found outside of Asia and Europe. To be sure, the scholarship remains to be systematically upgraded, but with English fast becoming the universal vehicle of Buddhist thought, there is no doubt that the American pursuit of Buddhism has already the potential of becoming a great intellectual force in the world. More than a mere search for tangible answers to life's ills, it is important at this stage to address ourselves to the keener aspect of the cultural dynamics taking place. The aspect is this: In what manner will Buddhist principles readily become a part of American culture? What are the specific principles that would make the greatest impact on the American cultural scene? Are there any signs presently that point in this direction?

The cultural milieu in America is always in a fluid, complex and, in many ways, unpredictable state. The ordinary mood of the people and the philosophical and sophisticated mood of the intelligentsia are different in a sense, yet they are both part and parcel of the total scene. The search for a common element or thread in the scene is indeed difficult. And yet we must somehow come to grips with the situation in such a way that some common focus can be made and a common factor realized or discovered so that all will be able to understand each other.

There is a clue here: if man is fundamentally in search of the most natural state of being, then the starting point as well as the end might well be in human experience. Human experience is a generic term for all that happens to man in his living process. It is vague in many ways and yet it is the common base and can be the common focus. Ordinarily, we are not really concerned about what it is, nor are we concerned about the detailed elements that go into it. For the most part, we accept it for the accruable results or tangible consequences. We are reminded of its occurrences and the many forces that are at play only in virtue of the visible so-called empirical elements. That is to say, we are captivated by those empirical elements from time immemorial and become attached to them. Nothing really spectacular or different or negative is happening to ourselves on this account that would make us re-examine our experiential process; therefore, we take on indifferent attitudes towards the empirical realm. Everything seems to be in the natural order of things; in fact, for many the natural is the empirical and vice versa. The upshot is that we become so accustomed to this rather prosaic attachment to the empirical nature of things that we hardly question it. We simply think, feel, speak and act by relying on these empirical elements. Such then are the set ways of life that we perpetuate regardless of whether we are attached to ordinary or more sophisticated elements.

What has been delineated is nothing but the school of thought known as empiricism which was refined in the British tradition by Berkeley, Locke and Hume. The empiricist uncritically takes as his point of departure a subject that perceives the objects of the world. Man's knowledge, of course, is based on this perceptual exchange between the subjective and objective realms, each supporting and relying on the other. Until fairly recent times it did not occur to anyone in the West that such an exchange was basically dichotomous of the reality of experience itself. Yet, empiricistic understanding is not easily dispensed with and, indeed, it is usually well received in most quarters so that we are never really entirely out of its clutches.

The historical Buddha, too, encountered empiricists of his day who built up their epistemological structures on the naive postulate of a self or an ego. The Buddha saw, however, that the self or ego is the result of a false metaphysical bifurcation and that knowledge based on it would only lead to further alienation. Once the bifurcation is accepted or, more correctly, sets in, it causes further widening and stiffening of the ontological situation. This takes on very subtle distinctions so that the one who is beset by it may not even be aware of it; nevertheless, it works in insidious ways which the Buddha attributed to ignorance (*avidyā*), a general term used to describe ontologically unclear perceptions and the resultant falsification of reality itself.

The empirically oriented mind "thinks" that it can mediate between the self and reality. This is, of course, erroneous, for the mind is one thing and reality another. The mind may be a "cleaver" of the passage of reality, but in the final analysis the "cleaver" does not or cannot "cleave" itself, nor does it leave its marks on reality by the "cleaving" process: that is, reality is not divided by the mind, nor is it manipulated and transformed into new realities. In many ways, the mind and its functions are accidents in the flow of reality and they leave no enduring substantial changes to speak of. Paradoxically, but inextricably, the mind is part and parcel of the very reality that it attempts to understand.

The Buddhist answer to empiricism is that there is more in experience than that which meets the empirical eye. "The empirical eye" means those elements or facets of experience which hold our attention and provide a base on which to build a system of knowledge. Such a system is true and cogent only to the extent that the empirical elements are absolutely true to reality. But this is a problematic condition. The Buddhist would suspect that there is something shadowy and superficial in such a system. He would want to understand experience in its fullness: there is "more in experience than that which meets the empirical eye." It means that there is a "reaching" or going beyond the mere empirical realm to show up the profound nature of experience. Looked at from another perspective, an empirical event is an event only as it is appropriated from the flow of reality. There is a selection, an extraction, a determination or limitation, and also the attendant conceptual abstraction of that which has been appropriated. Thus empirical events seem to be "floating," as it were, on certain aspects of reality. They are not, strictly speaking, *natural* to the nature of things.

The Buddhist would go on to say that experiences or empirical events are basically taking place in a holistic sense: therefore, nothing can be extracted and abstracted in the strictest sense of the terms. The description of experience is then in many respects "non-empirical," i.e., more than the mere empirical play of things. It must be cautioned, however, that reference to the non-empirical does not mean flights into the trans-empirical or extra-experiential nature of things—the bane of all mysticism and esotericism. A more detailed analysis of the holistically non-empirical realm of experience will follow shortly.

At this juncture, it is good to recall that the whole American pragmatic movement was one in which the holistic experiential nature of things remained constantly at the forefront. From C. S. Peirce, W. James, J. Dewey, G. H. Mead and others, the respective attempts to understand human experience had been guided by this focus on man in his total nature and surroundings, from the microcosmic to the macrocosmic nature of things. Man was an organism whose nature and function were set within his meaningful and manipulable surroundings. To be sure, the movement based as it was on the practical nature of things leaned toward science and its methodology. This became increasingly so between the two Great Wars in which one sector of the movement became so technical in analyzing human experience or the behavioral patterns that it lost much of the emphasis on the holistic nature. In the end such moves nearly merged with the positivistic systems that were spilling over into America from Europe. This is not to say that the movement had succumbed to scientism nor to say that it became moribund. The pragmatic nature of the average American's character is still very much alive and will be for a long time to come. Though other philosophies have pushed it in the background, this pragmatic nature is potentially present and ever ready to assert itself at all times. The Buddhist presence in America makes way for new contact with the pragmatic nature. In fact, the mere exposure of Americans to Buddhism in all its forms is already a clear indication that this pragmatic nature is being stirred or aroused. The crucial question to be posed here is this: Given the present ambience in a scientifically (empirically) dominated world, what prospects are there for a renewed look at our pragmatic nature? Where can we look? Is there a source of inspiration and accommodation? It is here that Buddhist principles or doctrines can offer suggestions. Among all of them there is one that is most relevant, penetrating directly to the core of all experience—the doctrine of *śūnyatā*. What is *śūnyatā*? What is its nature? Why is it so special? How does it manifest in human experience? We must now address ourselves to these questions.

First of all, let us examine the etymological nature of the term. *Śūnya* is derived from the Sanskrit root, *svi,* which means "to swell, to grow, to increase." *Śūnya* thus means, "relating to the swollen or to the grown."[4] It is swollen with respect to the empirical contents or elements, but it can be hollow or vacuous with respect to the absence of these elements at play. Consequently, what is swollen can also be empty in the detached sense; it refers to the full nature of being. And so *śūnya* in its abstract state becomes *śūnyatā,* the state of full nature of being or the fullness of being. Despite this real meaning, *śūnyatā* has been popularly rendered as emptiness or voidness or nothingness without qualifications and this has been a source of misconceptions.

We must expand on the nature of *śūnyatā*. There are several types for discussion but for the sake of brevity, clarity and understanding, the following two are delineated:

1. Apparent type.

This type of *śūnyatā* is apparent because it is not really experientially true. It may, however, have psychological and emotional values. This is further divided into two categories.

a. Metaphysical emptiness.

This has to do with the picture of the world in toto. An example will be the following assertion: "The world is empty." The statement is untenable except in a metaphorical sense, but it is apparent only to the mind that asserts it. It helps to give a monistic understanding of the world in terms of emptiness or empty state of things but monism of whatever form is not easy to advance, much less to demonstrate. It also promotes an extreme interpretation of emptiness, i.e., nihilism.

b. Ontological emptiness or nullity.

In this category falls the commitment made to an ontic nature of a thing or an object and that nature is said to be empty. Again, this is as untenable as the above although, admittedly, the ordinary person makes such ontic commitments, explicitly or implicitly, all too often. This ontological nullity is at times extended beyond the objects of perception and may even involve the subject that does the perceiving. But perceptual nullity or emptiness is a very difficult phenomenon to explain. Moreover, it is possible to include in this category all logical classes of nullity with which the mind functions. To be sure, such null classes do aid us in understanding logical operations, but they are true only within the realm of logicality. Experiential processes, however, are in many instances more than mere logical functions—whether negative, null or otherwise.

2. Real type.

The real type of *śūnyatā* is not empty in the literal sense but full and solid without any delineation as to substance or content. It is the *plenum* of existence or what I would prefer to call the ontological fullness or ontological *plenum*. Naturally, it has to do with man's existence in the fullest sense which, by the way, has always been the search of philosophies the world over, inclusive of the pragmatic tradition, but which has not been focussed on or addressed properly. We must concentrate on this real type of emptiness.

The obvious question here is, How or in what manner does the ontological fullness manifest itself? How does it "display" itself, or how does it come about? Among the philosophies of the world, it is only Buddhism that has really addressed itself to this status or phenomenon of experience in its fullness. Most philosophies have introduced so-called extra-experiential elements in an attempt to explain or cover up the phenomenon, while others have simply ignored the presence of such a phenomenon. The former is represented by metaphysicians who lean toward an eminent reality or supreme nature to account for the phenomenon. Examples of this are Plotinus' nature of *hacceity* which basically comes from the higher realm or Hegel's Absolute which eventually resolves all contradictions into its own identity. But these so-called grand philosophies only sweep the phenomenal natures away, and do not really go to the bottom of the natures themselves. There is simply too much unexamined logic and metaphysics at play which usually prey upon those who are emotionally, psychologically and rationally inclined.

Śūnyatā is an universal doctrine in Buddhism; it took, however, the early founding Prajñāpāramitā thought of the Mahāyāna tradition to take it up as a great force in human experience. Where or how it all began is still enshrouded in early Buddhist history, but we may safely infer that without this concept, Mahāyāna would not have developed the way it did. Indeed, without *śūnyatā* the prefixed term, *Mahā*, which means great, large or extensive, would not have derived its true meaning and force. The Mahāyāna tradition is noted for its twin concepts of wisdom *(prajñā)* and compassion *(karuṇā)*, both of which mutually support each other in the highest and deepest sense. In other words, it is just as correct to say that one who has gained the highest form of knowledge displays simultaneously the deepest form of love to all beings as it is to say, conversely, that one who displays the deepest form of love also manifests the highest form of knowledge. Both are, in this sense, two sides of the same reality of things. They are more than mere polar concepts for both have something more than that which satisfies the character or nature of mutuality. They depict the self-same reality of existence by dynamically implicating and identifying each other.

In consequence, there is something of a concrete embodiment in both instances, i.e., where wisdom is more than mere extensive knowledge and compassion more than mere affection for someone or beings in general. That so-called concrete embodiment is our central concern. By this, it means that there is a nature in human experience which is the "stuff" of all activities as well as that which functions as a "prop" to all activities. We are here describing an unique phenomenon, something which has not been related or delineated in simple empirical terms. It took a bold, innovative effort to not only come to grips with this underlying prop of existence, but to maintain it as the basis of sustenance, continuity and relief of the life process. That so-called prop is *śūnyatā*.

It was the great Mahāyanā thinker, Nāgārjuna (c. 150–250 A.D.), who first gave a philosophic expression to *śūnyatā*, taking the idea directly from the earlier *Prajñāpāramitā Sūtras*. He denied any false views attached to *śūnyatā*, the obvious ones being the metaphysical and ontological types discussed above, and challenged the ordinary mind to come to grips with it. He asserted that in the experiential process of things *(anitya)*, there are no substantial or empirical elements *(dharmas)* with fixed natures *(svabhāvas)* of any sort. They are simply empty *(śūnya)* within the process and yet, at the same time, it is obvious that the process itself is the only clue, the only realm, to which we must turn in order to understand the nature of reality. If the nature of reality is not to be treated empirically, including whatever elements that are attached to it, then it has to be treated in a non-empirical sense. The term *non-empirical,* introduced earlier, is indeed odd and unthinkable to the ordinary mind and rightly so because such a mind is not conditioned to accepting elements other than that which relate to the empirical aspect of things. In other words, the mind is captivated by the empirical nature of things and perceives them accordingly. Anything or any aspect beyond the empirical or that which is alien to it would immediately be suspect and eventually rejected or glossed over.

The emptiness of the elements must not preclude the fact of the process since the latter is basic while the former is ancillary to it. So that when we speak of the emptiness of the elements, the full nature of emptiness comes by way of the process as it is engaged in the so-called elements. Paradoxical as it may seem, the very empty nature of the elements spells out the full nature of the process. The emptiness, then, is not so much a character of the elements themselves as it is of the process itself. To emphasize or perceive the elements in and of themselves is a clear case of misplaced concreteness, to use a familiar Whiteheadian phrase. We must endeavor to focus our attention on the uniqueness of the process. By analogy, empiricistic understanding can be seen as the perception of only the warp and woof of the fabric. One sees just the obvious elements and thereafter the mind takes over and interprets everything else in terms of fitting all elements within the grid-like network. What can be "caught" in the grid is considered "logical," "rational" and admissible to understanding; conversely, what is not caught is rejected, ignored and forgotten. Over a long period of time, the empiricistic understanding prejudices against any rise of novelty and creativity, except on its own terms; or, what is novel or creative would be merely limited to the realm of empiricistic nature of things. The paradox of it all, if it can be so stated, is that the empiricistic nature of things is still expanding, reigns supreme in practically every quarter, and therefore maintains its great appeal and attraction. It is simply a vicious empiricistic circle.

Something is certainly lacking. The Buddhist knows the culprit and wants to put a stop to this proliferated state of empiricistic-elemental understanding. He wants to demonstrate the fact that the empiricistic understanding is patently shallow and only touches the facade of experiential nature of things. Following the above analogy, the Buddhist would point out that the empiricistic understanding does not take into account the interstices of the warp and woof of the fabric of existence. The interstices are, afterall, just as much a property of that fabric; in fact, they give a certain character to the fabric itself, such as strength, pliability and utility. In the same way, the wholeness of life process, the series of experiential processes, escapes us if the interstices of being are not accounted for or accommodated within the process itself. The empirical elements and the interstices are part and parcel of the total experiential process. According to Buddhism, failure to acknowledge this total nature of experience results in fragmentation of the most subtle kind and continues the round of suffering *(saṃsāra)*.

The clarification of the relationship between the empiricistic elements and the interstices of being opens up new vistas in human involvement. An example of primary importance is that all meditative disciplines in Buddhism are geared initially to induce the nature of calm or rest *(śamatha)* with respect to the empiricistic elements at play, i.e., to see the elements for what they are—as perceptual fragments within the holistic nature of experience. When this is accomplished, the disciplinarian goes further to seek the basis for the empiricistic elements themselves. At this point, the nature and function of the interstices relative to the empiricistic elements will be revealed by a rare insight *(vipaśyanā)* into reality as such *(yath-ābhūta)*. And that rare insight into reality brings us right back to the central concept of *śūnyatā.*

Only the enlightened, to be sure, is privy to the complete nature of *śūnyatā* and is able to perceive things under that aegis, but that does not necessarily mean that the unenlightened does not have the slightest idea of nor a feel for the nature of *śūnyatā*. He does in glimpses, but never in any integrated sustained sense because his empiricistic tendencies block off or eclipse the nature of *śūnyatā*. Eclipse, however, does not necessarily mean rejection or destruction. The eclipsed nature remains in the shadowy realm, so to say, only to manifest itself when the empiricistic elements subside. This then is the unique feature of the dynamic experiential nature that the Buddhist looked at very closely and understood. We thus can appreciate the twofold methodological nature of *śamatha-vipaśyanā* which is nothing but a supreme ontological conquest that allows intimacy with the true experiential nature of reality. In another sense, it is to have insight into reality as it really is by cutting off the rise of attachment to the empiricistic elements, for there are no separate or independent entities, no subject-object dichotomized ontologies.

Though the demands to become enlightened are simply too much for most of us, this should not, however, preclude our attempts to simulate the experiential process in all its fullness. And with this spirit, we proceed to explore and analyze further the nature and role of *śūnyatā*.

There are several characteristics of *śūnyatā,* but first of all, it is necessary to note that *śūnyatā* is not to be construed as equivalent to or identical with the interstices of being. Should that be the case, it would constitute merely another elemental offering to the empiricistic understanding and further perpetuate the dichotomous notion of existence, i.e., between the empiricistic elements and interstitial nature of being.

The basic nature of *śūnyatā* is to "hold" or sustain the empiricistic elements within the total experiential process. It, therefore, not only "covers" or "fills up" the interstices but also permeates the empiricistic elements themselves. In this sense, *śūnyatā* "absorbs" the empirical elements and brings them out in a better light, as it were. Afterall, the elements do not stand alone. In a more profound sense, it means that the process and the elements that are involved in it are one and the same reality in virtue of *śūnyatā*. In other words, *śūnyatā* is that which holds everything together in experiential process.

From the above discussion it would seem that *śūnyatā* is the potential receptacle of the empirical realm since it is the recipient of all the elements. The idea of a receptacle is an old one which the Mahāyāna employed successfully in describing the nature of the mind-function, the *ālaya-vijñāna*.[5] Nascently supportive of the empiricistic activities is this nature of *śūnyatā* which resides silently, but not in any underlying sense. The functional nature of *śūnyatā* is likened to the concept of zero in mathematics as it permits possible operations. As a matter of fact, the concept of zero is really an invention or discovery of the Indian mind, but was brought to the West through Arabian intercession. It comes directly from the concept of *śūnya;* it is not literally nothing, as discussed earlier, but in mathematics the zero can be nothing. The complete meaning of zero, however, must include both the logical and ontological conceptions. Thus, in the total (holistic) system of digits, the zero is a necessary starting point as well as conclusion; it makes all references of digits possible and at once contains them all. The *śūnya* of experience functions similarly. Being the "substance" of the receptacle of being, *śūnya* must have the nature of openness. Otherwise, it would not enable the receptacle to be what it is meant to be. Furthermore, the openness is not only an internal affair but extends potentially beyond the elements of the empirical realm, i.e., potentially in the sense that the sense faculties become completely neutral in incorporating their respective objective elements. In this sense, there is an open reach beyond the empirical realm which permits the experiences to function freely and holistically.

At this point, it would not be remiss to assert that *śūnya* or *śūnyatā* is the supreme ontological principle, the ground of all momentary experiences. These experiences, true to the impermanent nature of things, are empty; they are empty in the sense of non-attachment to all empirical activities and their elements as such. And this brings us to the interesting point that the Western notion of the "really real" must indeed be empty or *śūnya* in the Buddhist sense.

The early Prajñāpāramitā thought, crystallized later in the *Diamond* and *Heart Sūtras,* made the bold assertion that the empirical nature of things and the *śūnyatā* nature of things must collapse. The famous words say: "form is emptiness and the very emptiness is form."[6] This is perhaps the most cryptic remark found in the whole Mahāyāna literature, but it will constantly lie in the background of all Mahāyāna thought. Later on, Nāgārjuna will give the final touch to this thought by asserting in his *Mūlamadhyamakakārikā* that the experiential nature of reality shows up identical realms of existence in respect to the middle way *(madhyamā-pratipad),* relational (dependent) origination *(pratītya-samutpāda),* and *śūnyatā.*[7] It was the confirmation of the Prajñāparamitā thought on the way conventional nature of truth *(saṃvṛti-satya,* i.e., the empirical and rational realms of truth) must correspond with the absolute nature of truth *(paramārtha-satya,* i.e., the non-empirical realm of truth). This is manifestly akin to what Northrop asserted as the concept of "epistemic correlation,"[8] a concept that reveals the need for more exploration and re-examination in the light of East-West dialogue and understanding. Whatever the differences are, there is manifestly a basic correspondence which I prefer to call an "ontological correlation" which leads on to the "epistemic correlation." Confirmation of this thought comes immediately with Nāgārjuna's famous assertion that the realms and limits of *saṃsāra* (i.e., empirically attached life) are no different from the realms and limits of *nirvāṇa* (i.e., the non-empirically oriented life which issues forth release and freedom in the absolute sense).[9]

What has been presented in the preceding paragraph amounts to the capsuled essence of Mahāyāna philosophy. This does not mean, however, that the Theravāda lacked any indication of such a philosophy. Afterall, both systems employ the same core doctrines, such as the Fourfold Noble Truth, Impermanence, and Non-self. The previous discussion only points to the historical fact that the Mahāyāna developed its own philosophy by expanding on certain key doctrines that have to do with the experiential nature of things and thereby went beyond the tradition-bound Theravāda system. In the final analysis, it is the extensional nature, based on a wider, more inclusive concept of existential ontology as depicted in the Bodhisattva Ideal, that has distinguished the Mahāyāna from the Theravāda.

In noting the doctrinal equations made, such as *saṃsāra=nirvāṇa,* we must keep in mind that they depict the supreme nature of holistic experience. All of them are related to one another in one way or other. For our discussion, however, the one that is most relevant is the triadic set: middle way=relational origination=emptiness. The middle way is actually a methodological-cum-ontological pointer; it expresses the guides to focusing on the truth of experiential nature by not being attached to extremes of either substantialism (the *ātman*-view) or non-substantialism (the *nairātmya*-view). The truth of existence lies not in the moderate midpoint of the extremes, for no one could rightly come to such a point, but in avoiding both and thereby realizing the truth of existence that has no limits or borders and therefore is full.

Now, the truth of existence in its on-going creative aspect is delineated by the concept of relational origination, allegedly the most original thought attributed to the historical Buddha. For both Theravāda and Mahāyāna the concept refers to the popularly described Wheel of Life, usually depicted by the twelve links, that normally starts with ignorance and ends with old-age and death. The Mahāyāna, however, added a new dimension to this wheel by introducing the role and function of *śūnyatā* in a consistent manner with respect to the experiential process. The wheel may thus turn empirically, i.e., with respect to the twelve links, but it may also turn with the basic function of *śūnyatā*. In the latter sense, the wheel is actually turning without the characterization of the wheel itself. There is then the twofold sense of *saṃsāra:* the first is in the conventional or empirical sense, and the second in the non-conventional or non-empirical sense. So according to the Mahāyānist, true experiential process is *śūnyatā*-based. In the actualization of the twofold sense, we now could appreciate the equation: *saṃsāra=nirvāṇa* or *pratītya-samutpāda=śūnyatā*.

This equation simply means that the realm of experience, as it is, is still the same functional realm that will be realized in enlightened experience. Relational origination *(pratītya-samutpāda)* is thus a practical everyday concept which has all the potential of being "transformed" into the supremely practical *śūnyatā*-nature of life. Here we note that in Buddhism the naturalistic orientation is a fact in its own unique way for there is nothing extraneous to nor anything superimposed on the realm of existence. Nāgārjuna was the first to formulate this rather unique discovery:

> The Tathāgata's [i.e., enlightened one's] nature of self-existence is also the nature of this worldly existence.[10]

To exhibit simply the identity of the realms of existence relative to *saṃsāra* and *nirvāṇa,* or to relational origination and *śūnyatā,* is rather unappealing to the ordinary reader. Somehow, the identity must not be treated abstractly nor spoken of cavalierly. In order to give more credence to the concept of *śūnyatā,* I take the liberty to assert that it is more than a receptacle, more than the mere emptiness or vacuity attributed to it. In order to make clear its cogency, *śūnyatā* must in the final analysis be a positive force; it must be that which makes the relational origination possible. In other words, *śūnyatā* must be that which makes the process of integration possible. In this sense, I make bold the following assertion: in each experiential reality *śūnyatā* has the effect of cementing. In this sense, relational origination is really a series of so-called cementing phenomena. *Śūnyatā* is the basic ground for reality to continue to flow. It gives more "substance" to the experiential events because it enables the integration or combination of everything in a total, absolute sense. For this reason, *śūnyatā* again appears as the ontological principle or, from another aspect, the principle of holism.

The foregoing discussion on *śūnyatā* and relational origination prepares the ground for an inordinate interpretation of all human experiences. The Buddhist saw that without that ground for concrete experiences, all will be relegated to the frills, the peripheral nature of things. And it was the apprehension of this ground that eventually paved the way for the rapid rise in the developments of Far Eastern culture. Aside from Buddhist themes as subjects in the various forms of art (tea ceremony, floral arrangements, India ink painting, Noh drama, archery, etc.), experiences based in or on that ground have become a part of the arts themselves. More specifically, the concept of *śūnyatā* has provided the source for the depth and profundity of the arts. Whether or not the artist or artisan is enlightened, the quest for uniqueness is basically rooted in the capture, or even an assimilation to a certain degree, of the empty detached nature of things. It is to be expected that in the assimilation there is much of the formalistic nature that has come into play through the various art forms.

Since it resides in the category of the non-empirical, the nature of *śūnyatā* does not independently display itself except quite indirectly or accompanied by the empirical elements. To use a familiar Zen example: ordinarily we hear and are captivated by the woodcutter's axe chopping away at a tree in the middle of a forest. With an enlightened attitude, however, the sound of the woodcutter's axe is not only heard but, more importantly, it makes more obvious the silence of the forest! One side is mere empirical, relative to the senses, while the other side is non-empirical, i.e., going beyond the elements of the senses. The former is superficial and the latter profound as it delineates the depths upon which the sound "rests." The emphasis and the attitude towards the depths of experiences can be "trained" and realized in our everyday experiences. To be sure, there is a depth or source from which all is possible and to which all is somehow related.[11] D. T. Suzuki has said that transparency is the keynote to the Zen understanding of nature, and from it Zen's love of nature starts.[12] Transparency here simply means the perception or experience of relational origination as *śūnyatā*. Based on this perception, all of nature will begin to be seen under the aegis of *śūnyatā*. Now this perception is not only characteristic of Zen, but it permeates the whole Mahāyāna view on life.

For another illustration, some Far Eastern forms of painting are noted for the brevity or economy in their use of strokes and the lavishness with which space is left untouched. The empirical minded will naturally react strongly against such painting because he could only appreciate and judge it by empirical means and standards, in addition to decrying the waste of good space on the canvas. "Surely, there must be more to go on the canvas," he will assert. To which the Far Eastern artist will immediately reply: "But I have already painted too much!" The upshot of the dialogue is that the empirical elements are only signs or symbols depicting the larger nature of things and that if one could go no more than the signs themselves, then the empirical minded vision is still myopic. He will not be able to capture the spirit and content of the strokes or even the space that leads extensively everywhere. A stroke may suggestively be left half done or it may depict the beginning or the end of an aspect or movement or something else. But if the empirical minded searches for the ultimate nature of the stroke, he errs in that the mind has now entered to force upon a completed state, a patching up or coalescing of seemingly dangling empirical elements. For, in truth, nothing dangles or nothing is left half done or undone in nature; nature is always full and complete. It is a *plenum*, as it is, without man's intervention or manipulation. Moreover, we should not lose sight of the fact that nature is coterminous with our holistic experience or perhaps, more correctly, it should be vice versa, i.e., our experience is consonant with nature itself. There is nothing fragmentary on either side, although from our side, we engage in illicit dichotomies all the time in our *conscious* attempt to understand the continuous nature of things. There should be no attempt to unify things or elements, for we cannot do that however hard we may try; we should seek rather for the basis of the unifying experience open to us. Otherwise, we engage in abstraction or take things out of context from the continuum of existence.

Thus far we have presented various meanings and characteristics on the concept of *śūnyatā*. They are by no means exhaustive; in fact, they only point up the needs of further explorations into this most basic and fascinating concept—explorations that should only lead to more novel interpretations of the role and function of the concept in our experiences.

This then returns us finally to the main question of this essay: What are the prospects for the American involvement with *śūnyatā?* The answer, in a word, is excellent. America stands supreme in the world today. There is hardly a challenge to her in terms of involvement in the multi-valued cultural dynamics; she is literally the melting pot of the major cultural traditions. Just about the time the American pragmatic movement seemed to have waned before World War II, there slowly began a resurgence, an awakening to the international dimensions of things which reached the heights when America became involved in that war and subsequently in other bitter wars. While wars in themselves are destructive, wasteful and inhumane and should be banned from the earth if at all possible, there was one so-called redeeming value for the American experience that resulted as a by-product of the conflicts: the exposure to new elements and visions towards alternative ways of life. For the last forty years, there has never been a place comparable to America where the average citizen is exposed to so much, with such force and at such a great pace. Indeed, Marshall McLuhan's concept of the electric age could most appropriately be modelled after America. This does not, however, mean that the exposure to new elements is taking place at all times in the most propitious way conceivable. Critics will be quick to take issue on this matter, lashing away at the ills or negative forces present in capitalism, consumerism, life-styles, etc. Despite the negative forces, there is still not a single country in the world that could stand up to the massive pluralistic challenge faced by America. But in the final analysis, nations are made up of individuals. In America, it is they who are thus exposed to the challenge. The influx of emigrants from all over the world is unprecedented. It is constantly contributing positively and uniquely to the experiential enrichment of America.

One of the important aspects of the pluralistic challenge is that it is subtly keeping the American mind open and fresh and incorporative. In Dewey's sense, the days of the absolutely fixed ideas are over. There is simply too much mobility everywhere in physical as well as non-physical forces so that terms such as conservatism and traditionalism have become outmoded.

All this points to the creative nature of the American experience. To be creative means that an act is free, accommodative, integrative and whole. It must be flexible and resilient in the face of changing circumstances and conditions. It must, finally, be sensitive to its surroundings and continuous in its process of involvement. In this process of involvement, there will be tensions, conflicts, contradictions, rejections and sufferings, but at the same time, there will be acceptances, accommodations, enrichments, pleasures and values. The polarities are certainly part of the cultural as well as non-cultural experiential dynamics but they are also reminders of the potentially vast and great nature of experience itself. These polarities, both positive and negative, are awakening the deep consciousness of the average American. He is being tempted to be more sensitive and probe deeper into the forces of the dynamics. We already have abundant testimony to the positive effects of the challenge in the fields of art, architecture, music, literature, dress and food that have come from both Eastern and Western shores.

From the Buddhist viewpoint, actions taking place in America have the character of approximating or simulating a *śūnyatā*-oriented experience. We cannot, of course, be too presumptive. But there are qualities, such as, freedom, freshness, vividness, movement, rest, vision and value that are realizable only because of the "empty" nature in which plural elements are thrashed out, assimilated and embodied in the on-going process. The process, which is through and through pragmatic, is at the same time *self-perpetuating*. When a question is raised, as it must be, on the cause and nature of the self-perpetuating phenomenon, the Buddhist cannot help but smile for now the questioner is challenged to seek the experiential basis for the pragmatic act. If successful, he will be able to have a "primal envisagement" of the experiential nature of reality, thereby increasing the potentiality for his creative process.

Prefatory Remarks to David Lee Miller's Essay

The heart of this essay is the inextricable connection between suffering and joy that is found throughout the teachings of the Buddha, a connection that has been neglected in most efforts to interpret Henry Nelson Wieman to the modern world. Wieman's writings constitute a twentieth century presentation of the Four Noble Truths and an empirically committed Eightfold Path. There is the characteristic Buddhist preoccupation with suffering, whose sources are beyond the range of normal waking consciousness, and whose denial and evasion serve but to increase the evil and impoverish the qualitative richness of human life. Everywhere we find mankind's refusal to face up to the dark realities. The most highly developed scientific, technological societies of today are, therefore, insensitive to their greatest and most unavoidable need to free themselves from that hedonism which in one form or another has captured the lives of millions of people and whole nations throughout the world.

Wieman has the Buddhist confidence that through disciplined analysis and a broadly empirical probing of our entanglements, men and women can uproot the sources of suffering, overcome the compulsive confinements that resist all modification by evidence or reason, and become more and more open to the creativity that makes life joyful. As important as anything in this respect is the major emphasis of the Buddhist tradition, and of the entire corpus of Wieman's writings, that inquiry, criticism, and self-correction—particularly in the areas of our most cherished beliefs—must be made central if the bonds to the dark realities are to be broken and a more fully evolved personality find life suffused with rapture and joy.

6

Buddhism and Wieman on Suffering and Joy

David Lee Miller

Introduction

In his intellectual autobiography, Henry Nelson Wieman describes a joyful experience that was the decisive experience for the vocational choice of his life.

> Throughout high school and up to the month of April in my senior year at college, I was sure that I should be a journalist. My mother's brother was editor of a small paper, and in that unspoken way of hers my mother's expectations for me had become my expectations for myself. But shortly before my graduation, I came to my room after the evening meal and sat alone looking at the sunset over the Missouri River. Suddenly it came over me that I should devote my life to the problems of religious inquiry. I never had a more ecstatic experience, I could not sleep all night and walked in that ecstasy for several days.[1]

This autobiographical statement suggests an important but neglected aspect in Wieman's thinking. Wieman does set forth a kind of theology of joy. The intent of this essay is to clarify his emphasis upon joy; to show how it is inescapably rooted in the dark realities of human life; to describe the empirical method which Wieman holds is the only reliable means for attaining joy in living; and to suggest that joy as found in Wieman's thinking is at the heart of the Buddhist religious tradition. Wieman's view is unquestionably Western and in a basic way it is a Christian theology,[2] but more fundamentally it is a theology that touches the core of human experience throughout the world.

The experience of Joy

The crucial locus for the human experience of joy for Wieman is in his fundamental notion of creative interchange. At the highest level, creative interchange is the continuing process of joyful communication between human beings.

> Creative communication in its most complete form is never fully attained although human nature craves it no matter how much conscious purpose may oppose it. In its most complete form it can be described thus: You express your whole self and your entire mind freely and fully and deeply and truly to other persons who understand you most completely and appreciatively with joy in what you are as so expressed; and you yourself respond to others who express themselves freely and fully and deeply and truly while you understand them most completely and appreciatively with joy in the spirits they are.[3]

Each instance of creative interchange is an event, and "The creative event is so basic to all our further interpretation of value that we must examine it with care."[4] Further, the creative event " . . . is made up of four subevents; and the four working together and not any one of them working apart from the other constitute the creative event."[5] Wieman describes the four subevents in the following way:

> . . . emerging awareness of qualitative meaning derived from other persons through communication; integrating these new meanings with others previously acquired; expanding the richness of quality in the appreciable world by enlarging its meaning; deepening the community among those who participate in this total creative event of intercommunication.[6]

What happens then on each occasion of creative interchange between persons is (1) the emergence of new meaning, (2) the integration of the emerged meaning with previously acquired meaning, (3) the expansion of the appreciable world, and (4) the deepening of community. It is within these complex developments of emergence, integration, expansion and deepening that it is possible to locate the experience of joy. In the interpretation offered here, joy is at the center of the creative event analyzed into the four subevents by Wieman, and joy is what human beings experience when they engage in creative interchange with each other. The richness and vividness of the interchange is described aptly and frequently by Wieman as the experience of joy.

In his careful analysis of creative interchange into the creative event, further analyzed into the four subevents, Wieman is seeking to formulate the basic religious problem, which when understood and faced, enables us to seek maximum joy in living. According to Wieman, the religious problem has two features: "The one feature is man's capacity to undergo radical transformation and the other is his awareness of an original experience underlying conventional experience."[7] This radical transformation of original experience in the form of creative events yields the joy of living. This richness and vividness of living comes through a commitment to the creativity in events occurring through one's original experience.

> The ultimate commitment of faith in the religion of creativity is the only way to escape spiritual death when "spiritual death" means failure to live with the vivid qualities of original experience with the full exercise of personal resources and with realization of one's constructive potentialities and with a deep sense of the worthfulness of life.[8]

The joy of living carried by creative events receives special emphasis by Wieman in connection with sexual love and human history. With regard to both, the individual has enormous opportunities for experiences of joy. Wieman makes clear that while love between the sexes is more of a promise than a stable achievement, when required conditions are favorable ". . . sexual love can spread a glowing quality throughout the whole fabric of human existence and into every area of life, giving to all the world a joy underivable from any other source."[9] Human sexuality is a taproot of the human experience of joy for "Perhaps human sexuality, more than anything else, is what renders man capable of undergoing great creative transformations in the direction of an indefinite increase of qualitative meaning."[10]

At this point it is important to recall the four subevents that constitute the creative event. In the respective subevents, there is emergent qualitative meaning; there is integration of this meaning with previously acquired meanings; there is expansion of the appreciable world of qualitative meanings; and there is deepening of the qualitative meanings in the community of persons. The joy of sexual love is carried in the creative event and this joy is inseparable from the subevents of emergence, integration, expansion and deepening of the persons involved directly in the shared experience.

The experience of sexual love can reach heights of grandeur. "Sometimes a magic union of favorable conditions enables love between a man and a woman to transfigure the whole appreciable world. . . ."[11] Such unions of favorable conditions are rare but they tell ". . . us of what might be and whisper of a wonder that is hidden."[12]

Love between the sexes, Wieman continues, transforms us in the center of our original experiences so that "The sweetness and the magic of that touch may keep us faithful to a high devotion. We know wherefore we labor, having had that visitation. The hope and the dream of a world more fit for love shall henceforth be the goal of our endeavor."[13]

This sexual love ". . . means the capacity to be lured, transformed, and glorified by the depth and richness of creative interchange between people."[14] The import of the love is deepest joy through creative interchange for "When any man and any woman meet in love, the world trembles with the beginning of a new creation."[15] When this happens ". . . love breaks the constraints of self-protective concern, opening the way to deepest appreciative interchange."[16]

The joy of living can come to us abundantly from a proper understanding of and orientation to human history. "History is the supreme achievement of the creative event."[17] By this Wieman means that "At this new level creative power rises above the narrow limits of the single generation."[18] The joy potentially available to human beings is virtually boundless for

human history has scarcely yet begun. Millions of years have yet to run. Man is yet to be created in the fulness of his being. No form of life, so far as we know, has ever been the carrier of this creativity of history. Surely this is a destiny immeasurably beyond any other in the grandeur and tragedy of what has happened and in the glory of its possibilities. Each individual by proper action can become a participant in this grandeur, in this tragedy, and in this glory. To undertake such action is the decision required of us.[19]

Wieman's view of history is rooted in his view of creativity in events and joy is a crucial outcome of serious human commitment to this creativity which constitutes the basic meaning of history.

Creativity has found in man the medium of its freedom and its power on condition that man commits himself to it. Therein lies the joy and the greatness of human life for him who discovers this level of being and who gives himself over quite completely to the creativity of history.[20]

Wieman is confident that his view of history is much more important now in the twentieth century than at any other time in the previous history of the human race. "Perhaps nothing now happening is more fateful for the future life of man than the swift and irresistible tightening of the bonds of interdependence among all the peoples, all the cultures, all the faiths and nations and classes and races on the earth."[21] This interdependence plus our "magnified power and knowledge"[22] convinces him that the joy in living must come to us in a "history under commitment."[23] As Wieman puts it, ". . . man must now assume responsibility for the creativity of history to a measure never before required of him."[24]

If we do take this responsibility and make this commitment, we as individuals are direct participants in the joy generated by creativity in history. On the last page of *The Source of Human Good*, Wieman writes:

> History can give to all things mean and noble a voice to speak out from the past, bringing to the sensitive mind a love of earth and all things in it and the sky above. In this way it can endow the dying day of each generation with a splendor deepening through the ages.[25]

Wieman's emphasis upon joy describes kinds of lives not frequently experienced by human beings. In delineating the bright possibilities and realities of joy found through creative interchange, Wieman offers hope of enormous magnitude to the human race. In seeing the bright possibilities and realities of love between the sexes, we are able to understand joy through creative interchange in microcosm. In seeing the bright possibilities and realities of creativity in history, we are able to understand joy through creative interchange in macrocosm.

The issue to be explored next is the relationship of the joy of living to the misery of living. Wieman's theological emphasis on joy is rooted inescapably in the uncounted miseries of life. The inextricable connection of joy and misery is found throughout his writings, but nowhere is the relationship better explained than in Chapter Three of *Man's Ultimate Commitment*, entitled "Living Richly with Dark Realities."

The Experience of Joy as Inseparable from the Dark Realities of Life

Making use of knowledge generated by the behavioral sciences and insights provided by the Existentialists, Wieman offers a detailed account of how all joy in human living is inescapably related to what he terms dark realities. He formulates the essential connection between joy and the dark realities in the following way:

Dread is felt when the most beloved is threatened, anxiety assails when we are aware of a blessedness endangered or missed. The deeps of evil never reach consciousness, except in opposition to the heights of good.[26]

According to Wieman, we cannot live in joy without a sensitivity to and acknowledgement of the dark realities. Living richly is existentially inseparable from the dark realities.

All this shows that there is no way to live richly except in the presence of the dark realities. When we try to secure place, comfort, and happiness by concealing what we fear and resist and by suppressing below the level of consciousness our reaction to these evils, we impoverish our lives. The fulness of reality with all the richness of felt quality which it yields can enter consciousness only when we face it openly with our full capacity for apprehending it.[27]

Wieman believes that the greatest obstruction to the human effort to live with joy is evasion. "This source of perversion which keeps man from realizing the great good for which his nature fits him, can be put into a single word: Evasion. It is man's refusal to face up to the dark realities."[28] The darkest of the dark realities is death and it is, therefore, representative of all the other dark realities. "Death can serve as a symbol of all the dark realities because it stands behind them all as the last fatality, either the climatic evil from which we try to escape or else the lesser evil into which we escape when life becomes unendurable."[29]

Evasion of what we believe we do not want is then the source of the absence of joy in our lives. As behavioral scientists and existentialists of different persuasions also tell us, we deny anxiety, guilt, loss, dread and death at the great cost of distorting or losing the joy in our lives. The result of the denial of the dark realities is a diminished mindfulness of ourselves, others, and everything in the world around us. The price we pay for refusing to face the dark realities is the enfeeblement or elimination of the values we prize most highly.

For Wieman the way is marked clearly. "The more highly anything is prized, the more darkly do these realities hover over it."[30] The great values of life must include the dark realities, and Wieman is quite explicit concerning the relationship of the dark realities to joy.

A glance at the dark realities listed above will show that they enter into the essential character of everything which we seek and enjoy, indeed into everything whatsoever which we can experience. Consequently, when we evade the complete awareness of them, we exclude the full consciousness of everything. Most of all we reduce to a feeble flicker of appreciation what would give us greatest joy if we did not dim our vision to conceal the lurking evil.[31]

For Wieman the awareness of evils is an important virtue. This awareness of the dark realities is one of the requirements for maximizing the joy in living. Evils are truly and presently involved in the lives of human beings at different times, in different places, and in different ways. It is imperative that we are mindful of these evils. "No one can live fully and abundantly unless he can take into his consciousness what the whole self experiences."[32]

It is now time to look at some specific obstructions that beset human beings as they attempt to live richly in the presence of the dark realities. In addition to the dark realities of guilt, dread, loss and death, persons must contend with a great variety of obstructions as they quest for the best human life has to offer. Understanding and mastering these obstructions is crucial for the development of the whole self and it is the whole self, unified harmoniously, that is able to benefit most fully from creative interchange and the joys it generates.

Obstructions to creative interchange and the joys that it produces are basically outer obstructions and inner obstructions. The outer obstructions stand "over against creative interchange"[33] and therefore thwart the whole self in its effort to seek the development of the joy of living. Some of these outer non-creative forms of interchange are:

1. Deceptive communication—"This is the kind by which one conceals from his own consciousness and the consciousness of others what he does not want to recognize because it might break down his self-esteem or because it is dangerous or horrible or otherwise disturbing."[34]

2. Manipulative communication—"In extreme form it is brainwashing. . . . It is interchange by which one person tries to inhibit or suppress the thoughts and feelings of the other in so far as they run counter to what one wants to communicate."[35]

3. Reiterative communication—"In communication of this kind one does not communicate anything new nor receive anything new. He only gives and takes the signals by which the complexities of life are regulated."[36]

4. Muddleheaded communication—"In this kind of interchange one picks up all sorts of odds and ends but the miscellany is not integrated. It is not creative. It tends to diminish the range and depth of what

one can know, feel, and control because of preoccupation with trivialities."[37]

5. Other directed person communication—"In this kind of communication the individual puts on a false front which he changes whenever he meets different people and different situations in order to be pleasing or get by."[38]

Wieman's analysis of these processes that run counter to creative interchange is extremely important. "All these different kinds of interchange are woven together like so many strands of a rope. It is this rope, not the one strand of it called creative interchange, which can be called the social process."[39]

An important inner obstruction to creative interchange is inertia. As humans we use up, sometimes quickly, our store of available energy. Thus, "When weary, we are inert and unresponsive. We cannot undergo the transformations which a new creation requires. Much irritation, anger, violence, and destruction . . . can be traced to fatigue and frayed nerves."[40]

The joy that comes from love between the sexes exists always in relation to the dark realities of misunderstanding, betrayal, and death of the loved one. "The failure may even cause their world to lapse into evils too drab or too terrible to endure."[41] Various obstructions interfere with this joyous love between the sexes so that ". . . most commonly it is practiced as a way of escape from the problems and responsibilities of life. Men turn to love to keep the dark realities out of mind."[42]

A major dark reality surrounding the attempt to achieve the joy of creative interchange amongst all of the peoples on the planet is an inveterate and destructive nationalism, itself rooted in a diversity of traditions, languages, and values. For this reason alone, a creative commitment to history assumes difficulties of enormous proportions. Self-assured in affluence, power, and prestige, the highly developed scientific, technological countries of the world are largely insensitive to the creative commitment to history. Wieman notes in speaking of Western man (he should have included all advanced scientific technological peoples in the world) that "He is lifted on a pinnacle of power so high that he cannot recognize his own need."[43] That urgent need ". . . is that he be creatively transformed by interchange with other peoples."[44]

We have reached a point in history where the scientific, technological instruments of power are so great that a creative commitment to history is necessary if the human race is to continue. Wieman summarizes the necessity of this creativity in the following:

We have reached a point in human history where interdependence has become so intimate and so coercive between different regions, social levels, and areas of experience that interchange and integration of meanings must occur more pervasively throughout the expanse of human life if the story of man is to continue.[45]

Throughout the spectrum of human life on earth are numerous opportunities for joy through creative interchange, but with every opportunity is threat, with every bright possibility comes dark reality and obstruction. Wieman's point is that life on this planet is neither "pie in the sky" nor hell. Rather good and evil, creation and destruction and joy and misery are cojoined.

Wieman's main conclusion here is vital for it is a critique of all types of hedonism which are so persuasive in their lure; so dominant in their holding power over individuals and cultures; and so disappointing in their capacity to satisfy our basic human needs. No form of hedonism can meet these basic human needs because all forms of hedonism separate pleasure or happiness from pain and attempt to foster the former while trying to eliminate the latter. Wieman instructs us that this is impossible. Yet hedonism in one form or another has captured the lives of millions of people and whole societies throughout the world.

Secondly, Wieman's conclusion that the joy of life may not triumph now or in the end places a very special responsibility upon persons in space, time, and history to commit themselves to "what operates in human life with such character and power that it will transform man as he cannot transform himself, saving him from evil and leading him to the best that human life can ever reach, provided he meet the required conditions. . . ."[46] Wieman's answer to this question is that the empirical method of inquiry is the only reliable way to attain the best in living.

The Way to Attain Joy in Living

Wieman's theology is thoroughly empirical, and he believes the only reliable way to attain joy in living is to follow this empirical method. Wieman remarks that the influence of John Dewey enabled him to see the crucial importance of the empirical method.

Dewey caused me to see something I have never forgotten: Inquiry concerning what makes for the good and evil of human life must be directed to what actually and observably operates in human life. Otherwise, the inquiry will produce misleading illusions.[47]

For Wieman, the empirical method of inquiry is necessary if human beings are to have a chance for joy in living.

> From the beginning I have insisted that religion in great part is one of the major evils in human life because it is commitment to what men believe will transform toward the best but this commitment is often given to what in truth does the opposite. Consequently, religion based on belief not corrected by empirical inquiry is very likely to be an evil.[48]

Central to understanding Wieman's emphasis upon the empirical method as the only reliable one for guiding persons away from the misery and towards the joy of living is his conviction that "Religion like every other persistent and important concern in human life should be defined by the problem which it tries to solve."[49] Understanding the problem correctly is exceedingly important.

> What operates in human life with such character and power that it will transform man as he cannot transform himself, to save him from the depths of evil and endow him with the greatest good, provided that he give himself over to it with whatsoever completeness of self-giving is possible for him?[50]

The understanding and pursuit of this problem is the reliable way to seek the joys of living that come from creative interchange, but "this problem which is the primary concern of religion is very commonly misconceived."[51] Wieman discusses the different ways that this problem is misconceived and with each misconception the effective power of empirical inquiry is lessened, and the joy of living is achieved in a more haphazard way.

One of the most common ways of misconceiving the religious problem is to ask "Is there anything in reality corresponding to some conventional idea of God?"[52] The word *God,* according to Wieman, is irrelevant to the religious problem *"unless* the word is used to refer to *whatever in truth* operates to save man from evil and to the greater good no matter how much this operating reality may differ from all traditional ideas about it."[53] The word *God*[54]—which for Wieman is also a word for creativity—

is properly an object of ongoing empirical inquiry, and not a matter of trying to match an idea with a reality inside or beyond the world.

Another misconception of the religious problem ". . . is the assumption that the solution of this problem can be found by searching that body of religious tradition which happens to prevail in one's religious fellowship."[55] This approach is dangerous, Wieman believes, for it rather easily assumes ". . . that this problem has been already solved so perfectly that no further inquiry is needed except to understand the truth already established in one or in all religious traditions."[56] If the religious problem is solved and the solution can be discovered in one or more of the religious traditions, then empirical inquiry throughout the ever emerging range of human experience is superfluous. The extent and continuity of experiences of joy is then limited to existing religious traditions.

Wieman thinks that the religious problem and the need for empirical inquiry to solve it are sharpened by examination of the religions of mental illness and conformity. "In the religion of mental illness we find beliefs which are compulsive in the sense that they resist all modification by evidence or reason."[57] Moreover, the religion of mental illness is widely prevalent and ". . . not confined to the mental hospitals. It may be widely prevalent in the churches and also outside the churches."[58]

In the religion of conformity ". . . the individual does not cling compulsively to his religious beliefs and practices."[59] This distinguishes the person from one who is mentally ill. "But he who adopts the religion of conformity does not examine his faith critically. No valid evidence may support his beliefs and justify his religious practices."[60] Wieman thinks that the religion of conformity is extremely important to understand.

> Until recent times in Western culture this religion of conformity has been by far the most common. While not so widely prevalent today it is still the dominant kind of religion. Throughout history it has been the chief agency in causing individuals to conform to the demands of the social order and the ruling authorities. This power to induce conformity derives not merely from fear of divine punishment, although that doubtless has always been present. But its penetrating and comprehensive power to bring the individual into conformity arises from the basic human problem which this kind of religion attempts to solve; and in some form or other, however inadequately, does solve.[61]

It does, however, solve the problem much more inadequately than does" . . . the religion of creativity . . ."[62] Chief among the advantages of the religion of creativity is that ". . . faith is based upon knowledge gained by intellectual inquiry and tested by predicted consequences under specified conditions."[63]

At the center of Wieman's empirical method is observation. "Observation is the gateway through which truth must pass to become descriptive of actual events."[64] As we have seen, it is in actual events that the joy of creative interchange is discovered and experienced. Observation of what actually operates in human life is the basis upon which we are able to accumulate the necessary evidence that makes possible the creative trans-formations within ourselves and others that makes living joyful. In doing this we gain skill in distinguishing what is true from what is false and thus are able to see reality in events ever more clearly and comprehensively. In this way what joy in living we do experience is related directly to careful observation of those conditions most favorable for its emergence in our lives. Wieman summarizes the crucial importance of observation:

> We have tried to show that observation enters into all cases of getting genuine knowledge. We have glanced at knowledge of other minds, self-communication, intuition, and mystical experience only because these are often alleged to be ways of knowing without observation. On analysis, we see that they are not. Reason also, when attempted without observation can do nothing more than specify structures of possibility, which may or may not characterize events. Observation and experiment alone can inform us if they do and when they do. Authority, also, is no exception. Valid authority merely transmits to us from some original source the knowledge that we acquire from it. This original source must be observation and experiment or analysis of perceptual events.[65]

In addition to observation, Wieman places high importance upon agree-ment between observers and coherence as aspects of his method of empirical inquiry. "All three of these apply to every proposition alleged to be true, whether it is in the field of common sense, science, philosophy, or faith."[66] Agreement between observers means several things including ". . . that the observers shall observe the same thing."[67] Another meaning is that ". . . the two are . . . making the observation under the same determining conditions. . . ."[68] Coherence also has more than one meaning. Coherence means ". . . first of all, that there shall be no contradiction between the proposition alleged to be true and other propositions held to be true."[69] Further, coherence ". . . would mean that the new proposition under consideration would be one component in a total implicative system which included all other true propositions."[70]

The final significance of observation, agreement between observers, and coherence as basic aspects of Wieman's empirical method lies in their power as tools to search out knowledge which will contribute reliably to conditions most favorable for the joy of creative interchange. In summary,

> this threefold test can be elaborated into all the many parts and forms of human inquiry. But our present purpose is not to discuss the method of acquiring knowledge beyond a minimum statement sufficient to distinguish knowledge from what is not knowledge.[71]

It is difficult to overestimate Wieman's emphasis upon the method of empirical inquiry if human beings are to have a reliable basis upon which to seek the greatest goods life has to offer. He leaves no doubt about the importance of the method.

> From the beginning I have insisted that religion in great part is one of the major evils in human life because it is commitment to what men believe will transform toward the best but this commitment is often given to what in truth does the opposite. Consequently, religion based on belief not corrected by empirical inquiry is very likely to be an evil.[72]

As important as anything else about Wieman's method of empirical inquiry is its emphasis upon criticism and correction of what at any given time is believed and cherished by human beings. The process nature of events issuing in the joy of creative interchange does not tolerate any static state of knowledge or set of beliefs. In this regard, the hand must be able to erase what it has written, the mind must be able to alter its fundamental ways of thinking, and the behavior of the whole human organism must be able to adapt and reorient itself as knowledge and conditions change. The method of empirical inquiry makes transformative criticism and correction of humans continuously possible. The empirical method of inquiry instructs us that "Beyond all we know or think we know and beyond all the errors in our cherished beliefs stands the reality which sustains, saves, and transforms, no matter how different may be its character from my present beliefs about it."[73] The way to the joy of living through creative interchange is marked clearly with the necessity of criticism and correction concerning where we have been, where we are, and where we might go. Wieman explains, "There is no escape from idolatry and no escape from spiritual arrogance except by recognizing the possibility of error when one burns his bridges behind him as he must do in making his ultimate commitment.''[74]

This method of empirical inquiry as the indispensable way for attaining the best that life has to offer receives eloquent expression in the last paragraph of *Man's Ultimate Commitment.*

> I know that I cannot be in error in holding the belief that I am at least partially in error concerning the character of the reality to which I am ultimately committed. Hence I know with certainty that I am ultimately given to what is more than, and in some respects different from, everything affirmed in this book. With this triumph over error I make my last commitment: I cast my error, my failure, and my guilt into the keeping of creative and transforming power.[75]

The Wieman-Buddhist Perspective on Joy

Wieman's conception of joy that comes from creative interchange is an emphasis that goes beyond Western theological traditions to other traditions and peoples all over the planet. Wieman certainly thought of his theology in this way.

> Certainly I am shaped and biased by the tradition in which I was reared. The Christian tradition with its error, its evil and its truth, is my chief resource. Yet I strongly resent the current practice of appealing to the Christian and Jewish tradition as being the guide of life and identifying this tradition with God rather than seeking what operates in all human life to create, save, and transform.[76]

Wieman has attracted the serious attention of one, and probably many more, serious thinkers within the Buddhist tradition. For instance, "Ichiro Hori, a Zen Buddhist and scholar on the faculty of the University of Tokyo, judged me to be a Buddhist after reading *The Source of Human Good.* After reading my latest book, he writes that he joins me in religious fellowship.''[77]

It is in creativity that we find a basic framework for locating and presenting joy in both Wieman and Buddhism. Wieman's view of creativity as the carrier of joy has been discussed in detail in the first part of this article. The creativity as the carrier of joy in Buddhism will not be discussed. More than one interpreter claims that creativity is the key for understanding the meaning of Buddhism. Nolan Jacobson writes, "The whole of Buddhist philosophy in all its branches is permeated with this perspective on the creativity incarnate in the momentariness of life."[78] Guy Richard Welbon affirms that "creativity pervades both the way and the goal of Buddhism."[79] Herbert Guenther is in agreement with Jacobson and Welbon. Discussing what is real in the Buddhist perspective, Guenther asserts "Creative forces are all that exist."[88] Charles Harshorne states the basic perspective of creativity experienced between persons, discussed extensively by Wieman as creative interchange, in the Buddhist tradition:

> Sharing of Creativity is the social character of experience. Its aspect of sympathy, participation, identification with others. Moreover, even one's own self is, strictly speaking, another—as hundreds of thousands of Buddhists have, for over a score of centuries, been trying to tell the world. I hold that in this they have simply been accurate.[81]

Now hear Wieman as he summarizes the insight of creativity in Buddhism stated above by Jacobson, Welbon, Guenther, and Hartshorne, with special emphasis upon the social character of the experience of creativity. "Creative interchange is that kind of interchange which creates in those who engage in it an appreciate understanding of the original experience of one another."[82] Further, "The original experience of the other is highly prized because, for one thing, nothing contributes so much to the enrichment of any man's life as what he gets from the original experiences of other people."[83]

From the point of view of Buddhism and Wieman, the original experience of self and others is radically infected with joy. The foundations of the world for all persons and other living creatures are found in the power of creativity that everlastingly sustains and transforms in the direction of joy. We have seen that this is true in Wieman's thought. The task is to show that it is a basic truth for Buddhism as well. In this connection, Jacobson writes that "The Buddha's teachings advocate the exaltation, not the annihilation of the human drama."[84] Erich Fromm confirms that "Buddhism while rejecting pleasure, conceives of Nirvana to be a state of joy, which is manifested in the reports and pictures of the Buddha's death. (I am indebted to the late D. T. Suzuki for pointing this out to me in a famous picture of the Buddha's death.)"[85]

This joy that emerges from the creativity everywhere in the world can be found in both the Theravāda and Mahāyāna traditions of Buddhism. In Theravāda Buddhism, the joy emerges through meditation. Such joy has creative, "explosive quality."[86] Initially, "he who bursts every bond within, destroys its root without, and frees himself from the very source of every bond and restraint, he is the noble one."[87] In the second stage of meditation, "He drenches, saturates, permeates, suffused this very body with the rapture and joy that are born of concentration; there is no part of his whole body that is not suffused with the rapture and joy that are born of concentration."[88]

Jacobson reports, "In the *Abhidhamma's* intricate analysis of mind, moreover, 63 out of 121 classes of consciousness are associated with joy, only three are painful, and the remaining fifty-five classes are indifferent, neither pleasure nor pain."[89] Significantly, in connection with Wieman's emphasis upon joy, ". . . this experience is not confined to the person himself. In this stage of meditation the joy, friendliness, serenity, equanimity are, in moments of profound reflection, immediately radiated over the entire world."[90] For Wieman, too, the entire world is involved in this creative emergence.

> As history enables each generation to acquire a growing technology and a growing culture from the past, delivering them enriched to the future, the creative event is empowered to render more appreciable the deeps of quality in the existing universe and the reach of possibility beyond.[91]

Basic to the Mahāyāna religious ideal is that the Bodhisattva persists in the mission of serving as the source of redemption for all others. Thomas Berry explains that "this Buddhist relationship with others must include all living beings. It must be universal, completely unrestricted. If any single being is excluded from sharing in this relationship, then it is not soundly established."[92] Further, Berry continues, according to the Mahāyāna ideal, one seeks ". . . loving-friendship, compassion, delight in the joy of others, and equanimity."[93] This Mahāyāna ideal is strikingly similar to Wieman's interchange. Indeed, all of these qualities or states ". . . involve a going-forth from the confinement of a person's own emotional life to a sharing in the lives of others."[94]

In the Mahāyāna Buddhist literature, the joy that emerges from the creative foundations of the world are found frequently in beautiful poems. One of the most outstanding of these is "The Rain Cloud," a long poem that electrifies the receptive reader with its message of saving joy arising out of the depths of the creative forces which support and move the world. One part reads:

> It is like unto a great cloud
> Rising above the world

Covering all things everywhere—
A gracious cloud full of moisture;
Lightning-flames flash and dazzle,
Voice of thunder vibrates afar,
Bringing joy and ease to all.[95]

Buddha and his message bring the joy of creativity to everyone. Another part reads:

I appear in the world
Like unto this great cloud,
to pour enrichment on all
Parched living beings,
To free them from their misery
to attain the joy of peace,
Joy of the present world,
and joy of Nirvana.[96]

Much joy is expressed both in the thought of Wieman and in the diverse traditions of Buddhism. In both perspectives however, the joy is rooted inescapably in the dark realities of life.[97] This inescapable conjunction of joy and misery in Buddhism is one of the secrets of its longevity and transforming power in the lives of people everywhere. Similarly, the conjunction of joy and misery in Wieman's thought make him a major resource for redemptive living for peoples conditioned by the dominant Judeo-Christian tradition in the Western hemisphere.

The problem of suffering as the fundamental problem in Buddhism is so well-known that it hardly needs extended discussion. Quite simply as Jacobson puts it, "The major problem of life for the Buddha is the problem of suffering. It is the inescapable problem of every creature."[98] Following Jacobson's account the Buddha, like Wieman, ". . . has a very low estimate of life as actually lived, but no one has ever paid man a higher compliment than Buddha did in pointing the way to Nibbāna."[99]

There is a remarkable similarity between the Buddha's and Wieman's views of what causes misery in life. Basing his view on numerous Buddhist texts, Jacobson writes:

Suffering comes from wanting the wrong things, from wanting the things that do not make for happiness, from getting less than is wanted, and from pursuing goals that are expressions of suppressed and distorted cravings. Suffering comes from hostility, hatred, frustration, aggression; from dejection, apathy, boredom, and the interests of an illusory self; from following in sensuality and lust the pleasure principle which can rule only through repression of every other impulse; from the self hatred, guilt and restlessness that come from serving an exalted ego; and from doubt and uncertainty that settle into a deeply ingrained character trait in a person who is prevented in this way from going deeper and winning through to real understanding.[100]

For Wieman, too, it is the deep rooted compulsive behavior that blocks the creative joy of living and produces the misery. His description of what causes this misery is rooted in the same suppression, evasion, confusion and distortion of human behavior that we find everywhere in Buddhist accounts of suffering. In this connection, he writes that persons

. . . are inhibited and suppressed; they are anxious and troubled with a hidden anxiety which disturbs their dreams and impairs every joy; which impoverishes every experience of love and every experience of beauty; which corrupts every noble thing they undertake and reduces to triviality what might otherwise be grand. Three-fourths of their total capacity for thinking, acting, and feeling, perhaps nine-tenths, is starved and deadened. Their joy is pallid; their sorrow is half a mockery; their hour of triumph is shrill without any of the resonance of deep hallelujahs. They cannot love with the depth and power which transfigures the world. They cannot act with passions free and flowing in tides of power.[101]

Both the Buddha and Wieman saw clearly that the only dependable joy in living comes from an acknowledgement and a mastery of the suffering that is extensively rooted throughout life itself. Both agree that the joy of liberation from this suffering is possible in varying degrees, and both recognize, as Wieman puts it so poignantly, "All the dark realities can be accepted when we know that they are intrinsic to the creative expansion and enrichment of the appreciative consciousness."[102] This conjointness of misery and joy of liberation is beautifully illustrated in the well known Buddhist "Parable of the Mustard Seed."[103]

In both Wieman's and Buddhist thought, great emphasis is placed on uprooting false and forced thoughts, feelings, and behaviors. As human beings are deluded and driven in their lives, creativity dries up, joy turns into bitterness and the positive promises for human life turn into negative tendencies and expressions that permeate all of the foundational layers of the human psyche.

Buddhism and Wieman propound with great detail and ardor a method for dealing with the suffering, the dark realities of life. Despite the significant differences in the details of method, it can be accurately stated that they share the empirical method. More specifically, it is an empirical method with a purpose and that purpose is to increase creative joy in living, or put negatively, the purpose is to diminish the destructive misery in living.

In summarizing Buddha's approach to religion Huston Smith writes, "It was empirical. Never has a religion set out its case with so complete an appeal to empirical judgment."[104] Central to this empiricism is meditation, analysis and mindfulness. Jacobson states the empirical disciplines of meditation and analysis succinctly: "The Buddha's solution of the human predicament of the almost total and irresistible sway of compulsive drives and interests, is an attempt to make this power of mind accessible through meditation and analysis."[105] Both Jacobson and Nyanaponika Thera make it clear that the power of mind or mindfulness is very much rooted in the findings of modern behavior science, so thoroughly explored by Wieman in his attempt to delineate a reliable empirical method for guiding persons away from misery in the direction of joy. Jacobson writes "Self analysis in Buddha's teachings is based upon the observation, actually borne out in modern psychotherapy, that the painful symptoms of anxiety and suffering disappear when a person relates these symptoms to certain psychological conditions."[106] Similarly, Nyanaponika Thera indicates the radically empirical nature of the Buddha's method.

> The Buddha's mind-doctrine, however, is not restricted to a theoretical *knowledge* of the mind, but it aims at the *shaping* of the mind, and through it, of life. In that object, however, it meets with that branch of modern psychology which is devoted to the practical application of theoretical mind-knowledge.[107]

Wieman offers numerous statements describing the empirical way of shaping the mind in positive ways and stresses, like the Buddha, how utterly complex the problem turns out to be.

> If psychopathology has demonstrated nothing else, it has certainly demonstrated this. Men are driven, some more and some less, by unconscious propensities which frustrate their conscious aims and often lead to self-

destruction, to the destruction of others, or to the disruption of mutual support in social relations.[108]

For Wieman, the calling of the empirical way is a high calling that imposes a rigorous discipline and calls for a deep commitment. "The problem of sense experience for religious inquiry and religious devotion is not to exclude it; the problem is to develop it in such a way that it calls forth all the creative powers of human life in profound perceptions."[109]

Conclusion

In the Buddhist traditions and in Wieman's thought, the way is not to an imaginary Beyond of any type, but rather leads straight home into the hearts and minds of human beings. Alfred North Whitehead concurs: ". . . that religion will conquer that can render clear to popular understanding some eternal greatness incarnate in the passage of temporal fact."[110] It is something great, "incarnate in the passage of temporal fact" that Buddhism for more than two thousand years and Wieman during his ninety years struggled to make clear. They instruct us that life is filled with opportunities for joy; that joy is rooted in the wonder, splendor and mystery of creativity; that joy from creativity can only be experienced realistically and healthfully with a cultivated mindfulness of the dark realities and awesome suffering everywhere in life; and that the devoted practice of the empirical method is the only reliable means for experiencing the best life has to offer to human beings.

They further instruct us that the spiritual battle will be won or lost here in space, time and history. At this moment, there are pioneers throughout the world variously engaged in this battle. The outcome is uncertain. What is quite certain is that more pioneers are needed to help wage the spiritual battle. Jacobson is attuned to the pioneers who are committed to the creative foundations of the world out of which the great values of life continuously emerge. Concerning these individuals, he writes that "for the pioneers themselves, nature confers upon them only one sign that they have been chosen. That sign is joy."[111] And further, "where there is joy, there is creation; the richer the creation, the deeper the joy."[112]

The Buddha and Wieman have announced that the flow of felt creativity is the fundamental source of security for living creatures in this world. This flow of felt creativity permeates the events that make and remake all of reality. They have outlined in detail the obstacles that stymie and distort this creativity, and they have exposed the deep-seated sources of human propensities that drive us in the ways of lust for illusory pleasure, praise and power. In our deepest dimensions we are caught within the perplexing and heart rending wounds and tragedies of the condition of sensitive, probing living beings. We might and can, however, gain our freedom to joy in living through penetration into the flow of felt creativity that makes us more fully awake, perceptive and capable of kindness and mercy towards ourselves and others. When we make this penetration with sufficient empirical commitment into the creative foundations of the world, we are pioneers on a new frontier, capable of celebrating each new day the joy of being alive. Our struggles and sufferings then acquire a different and more hopeful perspective, a Buddhist-Wieman perspective which is essential to the rapidly emerging world civilization.

Prefatory Remarks to Richard Chi's Essay

In this brief essay, Richard Chi reveals, much to the chagrin of Western logicians, the early contribution on truth functions made by the Buddhist logician, Dignāga (c. A.D. 400–485). Dignāga was not only the founder of Buddhist logic but also a figure to contend with in the development of Indian logic in general. He dealt with existents only, not having the benefits of symbolic language, but his method was thorough and accurate in presenting the extensional nature of propositions. He came up with sixteen truth functions, something the West became aware of only in this century.

The monumental Principia Mathematica by Russell and Whitehead did not cover the truth functions and it was only after researches done by men, such as, E. L. Post and L. Wittgenstein that Bertrand Russell acknowledged their value. Still, he did not amend the work nor rewrite it.

Recognition of Dignāga's contributions is long overdue. In fact, Chi asserts that "the recognition of ideas in this world, whether on logic or anything else, does not solely depend on the significance of the ideas themselves, but also on many contingent factors irrelevant to the subject matter, such as, ethnic and linguistic differences." This is of critical importance in East-West dialogues.

7

Buddhist Logic and Western Thought

Richard S. Y. Chi

The encyclopaedic work, *Principia Mathematica* by Russell and White-head, has won almost universal acceptance as the most systematic and comprehensive treatment of logic of the day. It has been said to be ranked only with the Theory of Relativity. Such a thorough study, however, lacks an overall system and the treatment of some fundamental concepts.

One very obvious omission is a systematic treatment of constants such as truth functions. Some active members of the class, such as conjunctions, disjunctions and implications, appear in every page of the book, yet there is no indication about whether there should be backbenchers and whether there should be a definite number of such functions.

After the publication of the first edition of the book, new ideas were introduced to fill the gap. In his important article "Introduction to a General Theory of Elementary Propositions,"[1] E. L. Post gave the total number of truth functions of order n: $_2 2^n$. The number for order 2 should be $_2 2^2 = 16$. As a mathematician, Post did not give a list of all the truth functions, which should properly belong to the scope of logic and not to that of pure mathematics.

In the same year (1921), Ludwig Wittgenstein listed all sixteen truth functions in his momumental work, *Tractatus Logico-Philosophicus*. As a philosopher, however, he did not elaborate the logical technicalities of these functions. Extensive study of these functions was done later by R. Carnap, J. Lukasiewicz and others.

Russell gave his response to the new ideas in his introduction to the second edition,[2] in which he adopted Wittgenstein's "Thesis of Exten-sionality," yet he mentioned nothing about the formal aspect of the listing of sixteen functions, as if it had not existed.

In contrast to his indifference to the listing, in the paragraph immediately following, Russell gave overwhelming praise to the new invention called "Sheffer stroke." He has gone as far as saying:

> It should be stated that a new and very powerful method in mathematical logic has been invented by Dr. H. M. Sheffer. This method, however, would demand a complete re-writing of *Principial Mathematica*. We recommend this task to Dr. Sheffer, since what has so far been published by him is scarcely sufficient to enable us to undertake the necessary reconstruction.[3]

Apparently there were two alternative ways to make logic more systematic: creating an organic structure of all functions, and using one function as the primitive concept to define all the rest. Russell selected the second.

Using one function to replace all the rest is not only pointless, but also makes the process impossible. Russell's comment apparently indicated his preference for unity to multiplicity. In the transmission of message of whatever kind, there is a contrary preference, the preference for distinctiveness to uniformity. Using Sheffer stroke to replace all other truth functions in logic is like using bits to replace the entire English vocabulary. The bits may be able to preserve the information in all books in all libraries, but it is hard to find a human audience who can comprehend their meaning.

Moreover, the very reason why Russell selected Sheffer stroke is that this function alone, without the company of anything else, even the sign of negation, can be used as a primitive concept to define all other functions. This line of reasoning is fallacious because Russell has confused two different meanings of an ambiguous symbol. The symbol "p" has two utterly different meanings: either the naming of a proposition without truth value or the assertion of a proposition. There is no assertion sign merely because of abbreviation. When this symbol is used to define a Sheffer stroke, it definitely means the assertion of a proposition, and not just naming of it. Consequently, the Sheffer stroke can be free from the sign of negation, it cannot be free from the sign of assertion, even if it is merely implied. When an unabbreviated symbolism is used, we can see that there is no categorical difference between Sheffer stroke and other truth functions. In other words, Sheffer stroke is not a unique member of the family.

As a philosopher and a scientist, it is not unnatural for Russell to have a desire for simplicity, the "first principle," or "primitive concept." What is out of line is that his primitive concept was wrongly placed. The primitive concept should not be a member of the set of functions, but should go beyond it. Simplicity should be judged by the result of operation; a single primitive concept may not necessarily be simpler than plural primitive concepts. What can really achieve simplicity is the "tabulation process," in which not one primitive concept, but a few primitive concepts, are involved.

By the application of proper primitive concepts, numerous theorems in different branches of logic would become parallel or analogous. This would make the book not only more systematic but also a great deal shorter. Post mentioned in his article:

> Further development suggests itself in two directions. On the one hand this general procedure might be extended to other portions of *'Principia'*, and we hope at some future time to present the beginning of such an attempt.[4]

Whether anything has actually been done, Post's recommendation is a great deal more feasible and meaningful. Even at a quick glance, the procedure can be instantly applied to the logic of apparent variables (quantificational logic), to the logic of relations and to the logic of classes. At any rate, Post's theory is not limited to elementary propositions.

In all these branches of logic, the total numer of functions is exactly $_2 2^2 = 16$. The procedure of "tabulation" involves the following steps:

1. The "naming" of two arguments, which can be propositions, either real variables p and q, or apparent variables fx and gx, relations R and S, or classes a and b.

2. The "recognition" of these arguments, namely, "identity" and "complement." In the case of propositions, identity means the proposition p itself, and the complement means its negative proposition but not denial, because at this stage, truth value has not yet been introduced. In the case of classes, identity means the class a itself and complement means its complementary class $\bar{a}$.

3. The "evaluation" in which the concept of "value" has been extended from "truth value" to other kinds of values. In the case of propositions, the values would be "true" and "false." In the case of classes, the values would be non-empty, $a \neq 0$, and empty, $a = 0$.

The actual procedure of tabulation, involving repeated operation of product-partition-product, is lengthy, and has been discussed in detail elsewhere.[5]

What is amazing is that the extension of Post's theory to the logic of apparent variables or to the logic of classes may not need to be implemented at some future time, since it has already been done by Indian logicians thirteen to fifteen centuries ago.

Dignāga's *Hetucakradamaru* (The Wheel of Reasons) is exceedingly short; it seems to be an outline *(kārikā)* of a treatise for his pupils to memorize.[6] The treatise does not survive, and this short outline has puzzled scholars throughout the ages. Even in our own century, this work has been described by St. Stasiak as "mysterious."[7]

The outline is an extensional study of propositions. Its aim is to find out the right kind of propositions which can be used as the major premise of a syllogism to derive a universal affirmative conclusion.

Syllogism was an important topic in logic in Dignāga's as well as Aristotle's time, when logic was used as a tool for doctrinal debate. We are more interested in a broader aspect of logic; let us ignore its syllogistic meaning and concentrate our attention on the classification of propositions. Four stanzas from the *Hetucakradamaru* are particularly relevant.

Knowable, produced, impermanent,   (5)
Produced, audible, effort-made,
Impermanent, effort-made and incorporeal,
Are used to prove the properties of being:
Permanent, impermanent, effort-made,
Permanent, permanent, permanent,
Non-effort-made, impermanent and permanent.   (6)
Space-pot, pot-space   (9)
Pot-lightning-space
Space-pot, (space-pot), space-pot-lightning,
Lightning-space-pot,
Pot-lightning-space,
Space-atom-action-pot.   (10)

Not being equipped with symbols, Dignāga utilized concrete objects to express his abstract ideas. The stanzas (5) and (6) give nine pairs of properties $(a_1, b_1), (a_2, b_2)$ to (a_9, b_9). The stanzas (9) and (10) give nine sets of concrete objects as examples which possess either one property, i.e., $(a\bar{b})$ or $(\bar{a}b)$, or both properties, i.e., (ab), or neither, i.e., $(\bar{a}\bar{b})$.

Nine pairs of properties:

knowable	permanent
produced	impermanent
impermanent	effort-made

produced	permanent
audible	permanent
effort-made	permanent
impermanent	non-effort-made
effort-made	impermanent
incorporeal	permanent

Nine sets of examples:
space-pot
pot-space
pot-lightning-space
space-pot
space-pot
space-pot-lightning
lightning-space-pot
pot-lightning-space
space-atom-action-pot

What is confusing is that Dignāga gave examples when they are existent, but gave nothing when they are not existent. In order to avoid confusion, the description should be made explicit. Let us insert the word "null" to denote the slots where examples do not exist:

space-pot-null-null
pot-null-null-space
pot-lightning-null-space
null-pot-space-null
null-null-space-pot
null-pot-space-lightning
lightning-pot-space-null
pot-null-lightning-space
space-action-atom-pot

In the above, there has been a slight change of order in the middle two examples in order to suit our familiar convention today. Dignāga's order is (ab, āb, ab̄, āb̄), while our order is (ab, ab̄, āb, āb̄). The change constitutes only a matter of convention, and there is nothing in substance.

The first pair can be read as the following:

That which is knowable and permanent:	yes, such as space
That which is knowable but not permanent:	yes, such as a pot

That which is not knowable but permanent: no, no such thing
That which is not knowable and not permanent: no, no such thing

The nine sets of examples can be written as the following:

ab	$a\bar{b}$	$\bar{a}b$	$\bar{a}\bar{b}$
space	pot	—	—
pot	—	—	space
pot	lightning	—	space
—	pot	space	—
—	—	space	pot
—	pot	space	lightning
lightning	pot	space	—
pot	—	lightning	space
space	action	atom	space

If we use the symbol "1" to represent "there is at least one thing which possesses the property that," and use the symbol "0" to represent "there is nothing which possesses the property that," the above list will become:

1100
1001
1101
0110
0011
0111
1110
1011
1111

Unlike the classification of propositions in traditional Western logic, Dignāga's way provides a system which is non-arbitrary. On account of practical reasons, however, his table is non-arbitrary yet not complete. From the elementary mathematics of permutation, one can easily see that several items are missing. The one who completed the system was not his follower but his hostile critic, Uddyotakara, who preferred completeness to practicality. The system of sixteen was completed by the addition of the following items:

1000
0001
0010
0000

When the two tables are put together, they will become

1111
1110
1101
1100
1011
1010
1001
1000
0111
0110
0101
0100
0011
0010
0001
0000

This is the earliest "logical tabulation" in history. The table established by Dignāga can be called "existential table," which is to be applied to quantificational logic and the logic of classes. It is analogous to the "truth table" in truth-functional logic, which is familiar to every logic student of our time. The two kinds of tables belong to two different branches of logic and have different meanings, but they have exactly the same structure.

Apparently, Dignāga's logic lays a particular stress on the extensional relationship between two concepts, which are usually represented by the "middle term" and the "major term" in traditional Western logic. Unlike traditional logic which elaborates "figures" and "moods," Dignāga's logic does not go beyond the "Barbara" mood. This process is not restricted to "syllogism" in formalized debate; it is applicable whenever one uses a clause beginning with the word *because* to make a justification of one's claim.

Of the sixteen functions, four can satisfy the required condition: 1011, 1010, 1001 and 1000. The others are either inconclusive or contradictory. Any two concepts in the world, e.g., "democracy" and "freedom," "blue" and "furious," should have relationship belonging to one of the sixteen. An extensional analysis of the relationships would enable us to judge whether a given reason is justified. We are confronting influence peddlers everyday, whether political, doctrinal, religious or commercial, who apply false reasons for their persuasion. An extensional analysis would expose their fallacies immediately.

The process of evolution of logic is somewhat unpredictable. Shortly after Kant had announced, "Formal logic was not able to advance a single step (after Aristotle) and is thus to all appearance a closed and complete body of doctrine,"[8] J. D. Gergonne declared that Aristotelian logic had fallen into general discredit during the eighteenth century, "though still taught in some Gothic academies."[9]

Principia Mathematica marks a great step forward; it has been, as mentioned above, "ranked only with the Theory of Relativity." It does not seem, however, to have reached an Einsteinian stage, despite the immense ingenuity in every detail of the book. In the absence of an overall systematization through major laws comparable to Newton's, it can hardly be more mature than Kepler's physics.

When Russell commented, "This method, however, would demand a complete re-writing of *Principia Mathematica*," it seemed that he was not unaware of some inadequacy of his book. Apparently he intended to find major laws as breakthroughs to put logic in order; unfortunately, his choice was not the right one, and the rewriting was never implemented.

The real counterpart of Newton's Laws is Post's Theory, with Dignāga's *Hetucakra* as its avant-garde. It would provide us with a logic of logic, or meta-logic, by which various factors in logic—the constants (functions), the variables (arguments) and rules of inference—would be introduced in an orderly way. Such a work has not yet come into existence; the immense volume of the work alone would make it extraordinarily difficult, if not altogether impossible.

In the study of some fields, criteria have not been established for non-triviality and relevance. People in various parts of the world study one and the same thing independently, yet there may not be an opportunity for a dialogue between them. Moreover, the recognition of ideas in this world, whether on logic or anything else, does not solely depend on the significance of the ideas themselves, but also on many contingent factors irrelevant to the subject matter, such as ethnic and linguistic differences. It happens that minor technicalities such as "figures" and "moods" have been generally known in high school logic, while Dignāga's ideas have not received adequate attention even at the frontier of research. The history of logic, not unlike that of anything else, is conditioned by accidents. As a result, the evolution of logic itself, does not seem to be a "logical" process.

Prefatory Remarks to Robert Neville's Essay

Charles Hartshorne's challenge for a Buddhisto-Christian dialogue is here taken up seriously and with great zest. Neville continues the Whiteheadian theme of the asymmetric relationship over the symmetric and of the limitations of the substance-view where the concepts of identity, change and causality are burdened with difficulties. Within this context, he analyzes the realistic Abhidharma school of Buddhism which focussed on the status of the "own-being" or "self-nature" (svabhāva) of the dharmas and the attendant shortcomings. Neville goes on to say that the Mahāyāna, represented by Nāgārjuna, brought back and re-emphasized the basic nature of process thought to Buddhism. In the treatment of dharmas within the context of process, the concepts of relations (internal-external), causation (symmetric-asymmetric), unity and interpenetration (interconnection of all things) are discussed to exhibit the Mahāyāna concern for the rightful understanding of dependent origination (pratītya-samutpāda) and the arising of emptiness (śūnyatā). Nāgārjuna's thought as well as that of Hua-yen Buddhism are introduced to show the strengths and weaknesses relative to process thought.

Neville finally introduces his own view in accommodating the cosmological and ontological nature of things. He points out that Whitehead's view of God is weak because of his stress on the cosmological relation where the ontological instead should rule supreme in delineating the conditions of God in this world, i.e., the world's own "acts of existence." He wants Buddhism to take up the challenge by first recognizing the difference between the cosmological and ontological dimensions, where the former has determinate features and the latter indeterminate, and to seek the ultimate grounds for the creativity of man in the world. The creativity lodges within the "ontological context of mutual relevance," something which both Buddhism and White-headianism have in common and should discuss together.

8

Buddhism and Process Philosophy

Robert C. Neville

Process philosophy in the tradition of Alfred North Whitehead understands itself to be heir to a conceptual undercurrent in Western intellectual history. Whereas the mainstream of Western thought has supposed that substances are the basic elements of reality, Heraclitus' belief that "all things flow" has finally emerged as a commanding metaphysical position only in the last hundred years. One easily understands, therefore, the enthusiasm with which process philosophers applaud the Western discovery of Buddhist philosophy as a commanding metaphysical vision of process whose profoundest technical expressions are themselves ancient.

The encounter of Buddhism with process philosophy is of vital interest as well to the expanding culture of Buddhism. There are many signs that Buddhism's vitality in the West may rescue it from overcommitments to premodern cultures in Asia, just as in ancient times its flowering in East Asia offset its eventual subordination in India. Han China's civilization must have seemed as alien to the early Indian Buddhist missionaries as Western society seems to contemporary East Asians. The missionaries to the Han found a congenial resonance in indigenous Chinese Taoism, however, and Buddhism transformed itself in China to take on the naturalistic cosmic orientations of that Chinese perspective.[1] It is natural, therefore, for Buddhism to take interest in indigenous Western philosophies that might provide similar resonance.

Two Western philosophies seem at the moment to be of greatest interest from the Buddhist perspective. One is the fundamental ontology of Heidegger, very influential in the Kyoto school and currently providing a language for Tibetan tantric Buddhism in the work of Herbert V. Guenther, for instance. The chief point of Buddhist interest in Heidegger's approach is its epistemological, transcendental orientation. Although all of Buddhism has given some place to what in the West has been called the "transcendental turn"—a stepping back to consider not what is experienced but the character of experiencing—some forms of Buddhism give this consideration a primary place. David A. Dilworth and Hugh J. Silverman have called this intellectual strategy "de-ontologizing" and analyze it as a relativizing of cognitive commitments so as to avoid ontological commitments.[2]

The second Western philosophy of interest to Buddhism is American process philosophy and its naturalistic culture in pragmatism. In contrast to the transcendental orientation of Heidegger, process philosophy is responsive to those strains in Buddhism that interpret the epistemological critique naturalistically. that is, instead of experience being a second-order affair relativizing reality, it is a medium uniting subject and object in multitudes of complex ways. The Taoist side of Chinese Buddhism is precisely that interest which focuses not so much on the transcendental form of experience as on its content as empty, impermanent, and interpenetrating. This is the interest that finds in process philosophy a congenial sounding board.[3]

The topic of the encounter of Buddhism with process philosophy, therefore, ignores many aspects of the encounter of Buddhism with Western thought in larger perspective.[4] The thesis of this paper, however, goes beyond the recognition that different Western philosophies will be selectively responsive to different elements in Buddhism, and vice versa. The thesis is that the current encounter of Buddhism with process philosophy enables each to develop beyond its previous achievements. In the long run perhaps the developing "subject" will be neither Buddhism nor process philosophy but their encounter itself, with some as yet undetermined name. The following sections, though interpretive, will attempt to advance the dialogue.

Process

The obvious point of similarity between Buddhism and process philosophy is in the rough analogy between the conception of *pratītya-samutpāda* and Whitehead's conception of process. Stated in a general enough way to include most schools of Buddhism from the early Abhidharma to the late Mahāyāna, the *pratītya-samutpāda* doctrine expresses the Buddhist view of process to the effect that (1) nothing endures and (2) anything within a process can be analyzed reductively into other conditions. The Buddhist schools disagreed over whether there are any irreducibly basic elements and whether things have a moment of true existence even if they do not endure. But they agreed that the world as we ordinarily experience it does not present basic realities and that its character is that of constant flow and passage.[5]

Resonant with this, Whitehead's theory claims that process consists of momentary occasions of experience, each perishing as soon as it has come to be.[6] Furthermore, each occasion can be analyzed into its prehensions or feelings of prior occasions, which of course themselves can be analyzed into yet prior occasions, and so forth; there is no form in any occasion that cannot be traced back to some prior condition. To this extent, Whitehead's cosmology gives expression to the general Buddhist view. Furthermore, in these two points Whitehead stands in opposition to almost the entirety of the earlier Western tradition, certainly among abstractly articulated metaphysical views.[7] The main current of the West has believed that enduring substances must be postulated precisely in order to account for change, and that although substances have causes, in an important sense they can be conceived by themselves without reference to external conditions. So Whitehead's is the first fully elaborated Western metaphysical theory to which Buddhism could look for general sympathy.[8]

The price Whitehead paid, from a Western perspective, for being able to say that things have only momentary existence was a concomitant emphasis on creativity within each occasion. Each occasion is self-creative in that the change it occasions from an antecedent state of affairs is not made by the activity of the antecedent conditions but rather by the self-constitution of the emerging occasion. Once having happened, the antecedent states of affairs are passive and are turned into determining conditions by the subsequent occasion or entity that makes itself up out of them. Although some forms of Mahāyāna Buddhism articulate the immediate "thisness" of experience in language evocative of what Whitehead would describe as the subjective immediacy of becoming, Buddhism generally has no metaphysical category corresponding to creativity that could be internal to occasions. This, I will suggest, is an area in which Buddhism can learn from process philosophy.

Thomas J. J. Altizer, followed by David A. Dilworth, has argued that a more precise interpretation of Whitehead's conception of process is that it bears very close similarities to the early *dharma* theory ("elements of experience") of the Hīnayāna schools.[9] Whitehead's actual occasions, their constituent prehensions, and nexuses of occasions are "the ultimate facts of immediate actual experience."[10] Furthermore, with regard to concreteness, prehensions are incomplete by themselves, as Dilworth points out, and are abstractions from actual entities; and nexuses are groups of actual entities that are nothing more than the sum of the actual entities themselves.

Dilworth quotes Whitehead: "actual entities . . . are the final real things of which the world is made up. There is no going behind actual entities to find anything more real."[11] Like *dharmas*, actual entities or occasions become instanteously, do not change themselves, but cumulatively make up strands of occasions that change, and lie behind the appearances of the world of common sense.

Dilworth, however, goes on to associate what he calls Whitehead's "process realism" with that aspect of the Abhidharma that came under criticism from the later Mahāyāna thinkers. His argument is comprehensive and detailed, but its central point comes down to this. Whereas the early Abhidharmists had said that the common sense things of experience are empty and that the basic *dharmas*, the unconditioned *dharmas*, alone are real, the Mahāyānists had argued that even the unconditioned *dharmas* are empty. Whitehead is like the Abhidarmists in the claim that the actual occasions alone are finally real. And he is subject, in part, to the Mahāyāna critique, according to Dilworth, in his failure to regard the actual occasions as empty.

But let us consider this more closely. In what sense are Whitehead's actual occasions "more real" than prehensions, nexuses, or common sense appearances? They are the "final real things of which the world is made up" with regard to two points. (1) Their analytical components, the prehensions, cannot exist except in actual occasions. In this sense, Whitehead followed out and critically developed the Western problematic of the *res verae*, the true atomic elements. But this is only to say that whereas the actual occasions are concrete, the prehensions are not concrete by themselves. It is not to suggest that the prehensions are any less real than the actual occasions, only that they are real as necessarily contained in actual occasions. In their turn, actual occasions have no reality except as being integrated prehensions of antecedent conditions; from a causal point of view, a completed actual occasion is dependent on the creative drive of its component prehensions to find satisfactory integration. (2) The actual occasions are the only loci of decisive change, and therefore, are the sole grounds of the limited contingent character of things. This only distinguishes their function from that of eternal objects, for instance; it does not make the actual occasions more real. Eternal objects in their turn contribute the definiteness to things which might be chosen by actual occasions. Therefore, although it may be that actual occasions are more comprehensively *interesting* than other elements in Whitehead's cosmology, it cannot be said that they are more *real*. To be, for Whitehead, is to make a difference to something, that is, to function (at least potentially) as a condition within process.[12]

The situation is more complex with regard to whether Whitehead sides with the early *dharma* schools or with the Mahāyāna regarding the emptiness of things. Whereas Dilworth puts him with the early schools because of the common belief that *dharmas* (at least unconditioned ones such as Nirvāṇa) and actual entities are "ultimate facts," I would stress his similarity to the Mahāyānists because of the common belief that nothing, even actual occasions, has "own being." The heart of the Mahāyāna claim is that even the unconditioned *dharmas* are empty, and that emptiness means that the things lack any being of their own. "Own being" does not mean the capacity to function as a condition but rather to be a reality somewhat independent of conditions.

The heart of Whitehead's conception of process, I believe, is the recognition that the achievement of objective reality entails the perishing of subjective immediacy, with the occasion dropping into the past. Processive emergent reality is not "being" in the sense of having an identity of one's own, but rather "becoming." Within an actual occasion as it is happening, there is the creative drive to achieve a unification of prehended past occasions so as to be an object for prehension by later occasions. The immediacy of the creative process involves an indefiniteness regarding how the occasion can reach a determinate state. The resolution of that indefiniteness into a completely determinate form is what brings the occasion into existence. Prior to the resolution, the occasion has no being, only becoming; it does not exist, it only lusts for existence. This is why the instant time of an extended duration; whole lapses of time and change come into existence instantly. And having come into existence they are objective, finished past facts, available to be prehended by subsequent occasions.

At no time does an occasion possess "own being." When it is coming into existence, it is "not yet." When it has achieved existence, its own subjective immediacy—the only "subject" that could possess "own being"—has perished. The only "being" an occasion has is its availability to be a condition for a subsequent occasion. Is this not the heart of the Mahāyāna claim that nothing in experience has "own being"? If anything has "own being" in Whitehead's system, it cannot be actual occasions or the things they compose, for actual occasions are *subjects* of properties only when they are not yet; and when they have achieved properties, only other occasions can be subjects entertaining them.

At least with respect to the universal denial of "own being," Whitehead would agree with the Mahāyāna claim that everything is empty. There is more to the Mahāyāna claim than this, however, and it has to do with relations and causation.

Relations and Causation

Some people experience affairs in such a way that the enduring substantiality of things seems very important. Other people experience that substantiality as empty, as a puffed up exaggeration.[14] Most of us have both kinds of experience. Which is the truer interpretation?

One cannot argue, as Mādhyamika Buddhists might for emptiness or Thomist Christians might for inhering acts of *esse,* that the true view is that which results from successfully cultivated meditative experience. For, the cultivation might have been in the wrong direction; presumably a corrupt interpretation of experience might be "confirmed" by selectively cultivated intentionality. Nor can one aruge that there are two truths ordered as appearance to reality or, to quote Nāgārjuna, as "the truth which is the highest sense" is ordered to "the world ensconsed truth."[15] For, the priority established, whichever it is, needs some kind of justification.

Nor can one make a simple pragmatic argument that one view is true because it leads to salvation. Both views have been held by sincere, sensitive and intelligent persons to be elements in salvific experience. Furthermore, not only is the character ascribed to salvifice experience relative, in part, to the assertions of which are the true views, but also the character of the problematic situation from which one is to be saved. So whereas a Mādhyamika Buddhist might say that salvation is from the sorrow stemming from (misplaced) attachment to (illusory) enduring realities, a medieval Thomist might say that salvation is from a self-centeredness that causes one to be detached from the enduring realities in which God is incarnate and whom one should love. The religious question of course is much more complex than this, but religious success cannot be used as a simple pragmatic criterion for choosing between an interpretation of things as empty versus an interpretation of experience as filled with enduring loci of the divine.[16]

Claims with regard to truth, therefore, need to be mediated by the broad apparatus of philosophy and complex cultural experience. This was early recognized in both the West and in India, and Nāgārjuna's *Mūla-madhyamakakārikā* is as classic an expression of this task as the work of Parmenides or Plato.

There are at least two ways of responding to Nāgārjuna's chief arguments. One, expressive of the transcendental turn, interprets Nāgārjuna's intent to be the soteriological goal of causing people to abandon attachment to views of reality altogether. According to Frederick J. Streng, for instance, Nāgārjuna's inspiration was rather like Wittgenstein's, to show people that language does not refer to extra-linguistic realities.[17] Words are interdefined and inter-referring, and the attempt to see them as referring to ontological realities outside themselves is one of the main sources of self-deception. By use of negative logical arguments, Nāgārjuna demonstrated the futility of speculative thinking. Dilworth notes that this is partly true and that the de-ontologizing motive is strong in Nāgārjuna, but there also is a pro-ontologizing motive.

> Despite its rejection of ontological pluralism, monism, and nihilism, however, the Mahāyāna position is not free from its own kind of amb-vialence. A pro-ontological conception of "true reality" has crept back into the discussion. . . . A difficulty for the interpretation arises here in that this vivid pro-ontological claim is commingled by the Mahāyāna philosophers with their de-ontological critique of *dharmas.* They say that the Absolute is the *Nirvāṇa-dharma-dhātu,* the inmost essence of all things, the unconditioned, limitless, undivided, unutterable Reality. This Mahāyāna Absolute is experienced through *prajñā,* the "non-discriminatory wisdom" or "enlightenment." Needless to say, however, the experiential claim to enlightenment does not carry its own intellectual justification. The Mahāyāna tradition is clear on the point that such an appeal to "non-discriminatory wisdom" is itself a discriminatory claim—and thus as meaningless as other predications about the Absolute within the relative order of discourse. . . . Nāgārjuna's dialectical logic of negations is designed to free the mind up from intellectual discriminations, and thus to reinforce the religious way-farer's appreciation of the possibility of attaining the fruition of the yogic experience in his/her own awakening.[18]

Acknowledging the inconsistency of Nāgārjuna's position, however, Dilworth wants to reassert it again on a higher level by claiming that all speculative thought takes place within paradigms, that Nāgārjuna's paradigm is one among several, and that none can be asserted as preferable except from the standpoint of yet another arbitrary paradigm.[19]

But is it the case that all speculative paradigms are arbitrary and relative? At the very least we can consciously move from one to the other, with a continuity in cross-paradigmatic thinking that is not itself immediately reducible to any of the paradigms crossed. And in various practical senses we approve certain paradigms over others because of the fruitfulness of their interpretation of experience. This would seem logically impossible if the only factors were brute experiential data pre-formed by a given paradigm's categories, and the paradigm itself; in this case all thinking and experience would be dictated in form by a given paradigm. But many diverse factors contribute to the forms of experience, at many levels including the theoretical. One of the most forceful contributors of form is the need to make *prima facie* sense of ordinary experience, in particular of the causal factors in nature and in human effort, and of change generally. Now it may be the case that causation and change are inherently irrational. But if a theory can be proposed that renders them rational, is not that paradigm to be preferred to those according to which they are irrational? Whatever would be the justification for rejecting a theory if not that it is irrational to accept it?[20]

The answer sometimes offered to that rhetorical question is that the whole business of theories or paradigms is a mistaken enterprise, that speculative theories about the nature of the world are inherently misguided. But then, if someone were to propose a theory that does not lead to egregious logical or practical difficulty, and could couple that with a theory about how theories interpret the nature of reality, would not the speculative enterprise have made a straightforward advance?

That is precisely what process philosophy claims to have done.[21] According to process philosophy, the reason for both the ancient Buddhist and the contemporary transcendental interest in denying the validity of specualtive metaphysics is that they suffered from impoverished metaphysical ideas. With improved ideas that there should be no such anti-speculative or de-ontological motive. (That soteriological interests require de-ontologizing will be criticized later.)

Let us then review the problem with respect to Nāgārjuna and Whitehead. In the first two chapters of the *Mūlamadhyamakakārikā,* Nāgārjuna attacked the conceptions of conditioning causes and of change, showing that upon certain assumptions of what they must be, they are impossible. Does his negative argument apply to process philosophy's conception of causation and change?

To be more specific about the Whiteheadian process philosophy, an occasion of experience (or an actual entity) comes to be with both passive and active factors. The previous actual occasions are objects to be prehended or felt by the emerging occasion; although they do not act, they constitute the given initial data from which the new occasion emerges through transforming, eliminating and/or integrating them. Each set of data has various possibilities of integration to which the emerging occasion must conform. But the activity of the actual integration, by which the initial data are transformed into a pattern which satisfies the requirements of integrity, is the creative self-constitution of the emerging occasion; this is the active factor. The previous occasions are conditions for the emerging occasion, but the emerging occasion itself makes those previous occasions into conditions by incorporating them in its integral nature, objectified for subsequent prehension. And the emerging occasion in some cases has considerable leeway as to what role the antecedent conditions will play in its own constitution. (The crucial factor in Whitehead's analysis which is lacking in the Buddhist analysis is the creativity exercised within each occasion's coming to be.)

To turn to a discussion of Nāgārjuna, he argued, first, that a cause can neither possess its own cause nor can it not possess its own cause.[22] For process philosophy, however, a cause in one sense possesses its own causes in that it incorporates them into its own integral reality, enjoying them as their subject; in another sense it does not possess them because they are objective for it, their own subjective reality having passed away when they achieved their own satisfactory integrity.

Next Nāgārjuna argued that a conditioning cause is such only when that which it conditions comes upon them, but that it would not have existed before conditioning anything. Furthermore, when the conditioning cause exists, its effect is not yet, and when its effect exists, the cause has passed away.[23] But this is no paradox for process philosophy. The subjective reality (the reality as subject of experience) of a condition passes away when it achieves objectivity, and it has objectivity in the sense of being available for prehension ever after. But it does not actually condition anything until prehended into a new occasion. Whereas the subjective reality of the condition passes away, its objective reality is everlasting, and its efficacy as a condition depends on the subjective creativity of subsequent prehending occasions, not on any impoverished life of its own.

Nāgārjuna said, "If an element occurs which is neither real nor non-real nor both real-and-non-real, how can there be a cause which is effective in this situation?"[24] If the element is a Whiteheadian occasion it is subjectively real and objectively non-real in its occurrence, and subjectively non-real and objectively real when it has achieved satisfaction. An antecedent cause for that occasion can not be effective creatively in the coming to be of the occasion, because all efficacy of that sort belongs to the subjective life of the emergent. But it can be effective in the sense of a resource and determining limit. If the condition is objectified by the emerging occasion, then it is effective yet beyond the first occasion it conditions. Nāgārjuna said, "Just that which is without an object of sensation is accepted as a real element; then if there is an element having no object of sensation, how is it possible to have an object of sensation?"[25] Whitehead would answer that a conditioning cause in itself is an objective datum, possibly with no intentional character to it. But when it is prehended, the form by which it is integrated with other things prehended may be such that it functions propositionally as an object of intention. Being an object of intention does not entail being intentional (or mental), because intentionality is a function of subjective form of its being prehended.

If an element has appeared and disappeared, said Nāgārjuna, then there could be no immediately preceding cause of it, for if there were the cause, it would not have ceased.[26] But since, for process philosophy, what "arises and falls" with respect to *dharmas* is the subjective immediacy of their self-creative coming to be, and since this self-creativity is unique to each thing, an immediately preceding cause must have disappeared subjectively in order to be an objective condition. The effectiveness of the condition is temporary with respect to its being grasped by the self-creativity in the coming to be of the effect, and once the effect has reached its own integration, both the immediately preceding cause and the newly finished effect are objectively immortal as potential conditions for further occasions.

If a thing derives its existence from another, said Nāgārjuna, then it has no existence of its own and hence cannot exist.[27] For Whitehead, the subjective existential activity producing an integrated new datum is an occasion's own self-creativity, which is not derived from anything else. But the conditions integrated are derived from past acts of creativity, and are the objective data. The objective data of the past are carried forward insofar as the new occasion does not eliminate or transform them but objectifies them in its own satisfied integration.

If the product does not reside in its causes, asked Nāgārjuna, how can it result from them?[28] Process philosophy answers that the antecedent occasions are the conditions making up the product, but the subjective reality of making up the product derives from the product's own self-creative act of integrating the antecedents.

Since a product consists of its conditioning causes, said Nāgārjuna, and since those causes in turn consist of their own causes, indefinitum, how can anything come to be a product?[29] By the fact, answers process philosophy, that each occasion in the causal chain constitutes its own novel subjective reality out of whatever antecedents it has by its own creative act. No thing could come to be without antecedents, since it would have nothing to integrate. But the antecedents alone do not cause the *sui generis* occasion.

If a condition does not produce its effect, how can it cause (or non-cause) when no product is produced? asked Nāgārjuna.[30] Products are produced out of the conditions, however, by their own creativity. The conditions cause by being taken up into the new occasion. If no occasion takes them up, they are no less objective and available for prehension than otherwise.

Nāgārjuna's analysis of motion or "going to" in Chapter 2 can be dealt with more briefly. There is no motion without that which moves, he said, yet that which moves is not a mover without moving. Further, no motion takes place except insofar as movement is achieved; yet once the motion is achieved there is no more moving. This is a familiar Western theme for which process philosophy has a clear alternative treatment. The subject of an occasion itself emerges as the integration within its coming to be taken place. There is no agent in an occasion doing the integration; rather, the occasion is the arising of a new integration which is the emergent entity. The sense of motion involved in coming to be is not existent motion, for only the achieved change from an antecedent conditions "exists." It is rather simply a subjective coming to be of an objective new datum. Existent motion, on the other hand, is the measurable change from the antecedent conditions to the situation with the newly emerged occasion. Any talk of agents which move must refer not to individual occasions but to trains of objectified emerged occasions. The subjective immediacy of coming to be is not something done by agent movers but is the emergence of subjects of the integration process.

Nāgārjuna's other arguments concerning the reality of *dharmas* and other features of the world depend similarly upon criticizing positions unlike the process cosmology. Since the process cosmology can give *prima facie* explanation of them (or at least of causation and motion) it is immune from his attack and one therefore cannot conclude that speculative views are all false.

Dilworth interprets the situation as follows. Nāgārjuna, like F. H. Bradley, assumes that any real relation must be an internal one. So for instance the product must be *in* the cause or it is not related to the cause at all. Whitehead, however, said that subsequent prehending occasions are external to the objective constitution of the conditions, although the conditions are internal to the prehending effects. Dilworth puts them down to a mere difference in paradigm. But this obscures the logical situation.

Why would Nāgārjuna or Bradley believe that all relations must be symmetrically internal? Either they could not think of a logical alternative, such as the asymmetrical view of Whitehead's, or they thought the symmetrically internal relations view better interprets the phenomena. But Whitehead's theory is indeed a logical alternative (unless someone shows it to be contradictory), and it does not require one to say paradoxical things about causation, motion, and the like.

Of course, there is no reason to suspect that Whitehead's theory is anything more certain than an hypothesis that is dialectically superior to a finite set of alternatives; surely one day it shall be improved upon. But it does not seem to be superior to the theory Nāgārjuna showed to be paradoxical. Hence Nāgārjuna's claim to have proved all *dharmas* empty in the sense of their being self-contradictory is unjustified. We can, in fact, entertain a cosmological theory of process that interprets basic categories such as causation and motion with *prima facie* plausibility. As remarked in the earlier section, this process cosmology allows that things are empty in the sense of not having any own-being; but it does not allow that speculative thinking must be misguided, contradictory, or erroneous. The transcendental interpretation of Nāgārjuna is not as interesting as the ontological interpretation. If Nāgārjuna objected to speculative thinking, it should not have been on intrinsic grounds, as his apparently logical arguments allege. The objection would have to be based on other, perhaps soteriological, grounds.

Streng interprets the positive side of Nāgārjuna's vision as an articulation of the interconnectedness of all things. Sūnyatā, he suggests, can be translated, following Stcherbatsky, as "relativity."[31] Rather than allowing metaphysical theories to stand in between ourselves and the world, especially other people, we should see our language merely as the medium making the connection.

The conclusion of this part of the discussion is that, although process philosophy agrees that process is empty, it disputes that strain in Buddhism which would say process is illusory or that theories asserting and interpreting the causal flow are logically inappropriate. Nāgārjuna's refutation of causation and change fails with respect to the contributions of process philosophy.

Unity and Interpenetration

Thomas J. J. Altizer, while likening Whitehead's theory of process to the early *dharma* theory, points out that Whitehead's greatest parallel with

Buddhism lies in his religious vision of the interconnection of all things. In perhaps the most imaginative treatment of the encounter of process philosophy and Buddhism to date, Altizer notes that Whitehead and Mahāyāna Buddhism uniquely identify the factual and the religious, and that both characterize the religiously ultimate elements in terms of interrelation and the coincidence of opposites.

Whitehead was fundamentally a religious thinker, in Altizer's view, but the imaginative ground for the Whiteheadian religious vision is not to be found in the West. The West, for Altizer, has been ineluctably wed to conceptualities of transcendence, dichotomizing God and nature, sacred and profane, real and apparent. Rather, the imaginative ground for Whitehead's vision is to be found in Buddhism, not in Christianity. Not that Whitehead learned his vision from Buddhism, but that his vision is uniquely available and publically penetrable through the language and imagery of Buddhism.[32]

Altizer's remarks in fact suggest a different way of interpreting Nāgārjuna. Whereas the particular symmetrical internal relations theory attacked by Nāgārjuna accentuated dichotomies and the transcendence of the genuinely religious from the flowing world, the destruction of that theory and its way of thinking allows the spiritual dimension to appear in the immediacy of fact. This might have been Nāgārjuna's intent. As Dilworth points out, this is what the yogic experience was supposed to reveal.

In light of the previous discussion of process and *pratītya-samutpāda*, however, two new complexities arise regarding the parallel between Buddhism and Whitehead on interrelation. The first arises from a point best made by Altizer.

Already in *Religion in the Making* Whitehead says that the realization of the togetherness or the interdependence of the universe is the contribution of religion to metaphysics. . . . Cosmic relatedness is the core of Whitehead's cosmology, which is concerned with the becoming, the being, and the relatedness of what he terms actual entities. . . . Whitehead believed that "everlastingness" (the "many" absorbed everlastingly in the final unity) is the actual content out of which the higher religions historically evolved. Now in this context it might be instructive to examine Whitehead's doctrine that the salvation of reality lies in its obstinate, irreducible, matter-of-fact entities. Is this doctrine grounded in a religious apprehension of the togetherness of the universe, leading to an understanding of actuality as complete togetherness? . . . What else but a religious vision could not only make manifest the totality of the interrelatedness of the universe but also unveil the intrinsic and even total interrelatedness of matter-of-fact entities? Do we not find lying at the center of Whitehead's vision a nondualistic apprehension of the union or coinherence of the macrocosmic and the microcosmic, of the outer and the inner, of the beyond and the near at hand which has no genuine precedent in the Western historical tradition?[33]

It is the religious vision of interrelatedness that Altizer finds to have imaginative grounding in Buddhism but not in the Western imagination.

Unfortunately, this interpretation of Whitehead is incomplete. First of all, with regard to the existential coming to be of things, occasions are entirely separate from contemporaries. They prehend only the finished past, and can be prehended only by future occasions when they themselves have perished in their subjective immediacy. The cosmic interelatedness, therefore, pertains only to occasions that are finished insofar as they are objectively resident in other prehending subjects. Whitehead's conception of God provides a model by which all things that are finished can be prehended without loss and, once they have occurred, are everlasting in the experience of God. But this leaves out of relation both the immediacy of occasion's existence and their projections toward the future which, if they are related, are only potentially so.[34] Second, because it requires a separate act of self-creation for one occasion to be a subject entertaining other occasions in an interrelated way, this aspect of Whitehead's theory is ineluctibly dualistic. With respect to the doctrine that God is the everlasting subject making it possible for each fleeting occasion of the world to be entertained immortally, the finitude and over-against-ness of God leads to a dualism even stronger than the Western theories representing God as a higher principle in which finite things participate. Alitzer would interpret Whitehead as using God-language to speak forth a Buddhist perspective and not a doctrine of a transcendent God at all. Yet if one eliminates those elements from Whitehead's philosophical theology that set God off as an other over against the world, one also eliminates those elements allowing for cosmic interrelatedness. Process philosophy must find a different conceptuality from its theism to articulate Whitehead's and Buddhism's aesthetic of interre-latedness, a problem to which we shall return.

The second complexity for interrelation and process philosophy builds on the first. As mentioned before, process philosophy's conception of causation is asymmetrical. That is, the later moments, are in part external to the earlier ones, while the earlier ones are internal to the later ones that prehend them. Interrelation is thus a function of earlier moments being prehended into unity by later moments or by God in the divine consequent nature. Temporal flow is fully real, for process philosophy, not only in the subjective immediacy of coming to be, but in the characters of relations between temporal moments. This stands in contrast to the scale of interrelatedness in at least one school of Mahāyāna Buddhism, the Hua-yen. Hua-yen's distinctive contribution has been its elaboration of the doctrine of mutual interpenetration.

In his *The Buddhist Teaching of Totality*, Garma C. C. Chang notes the similarity of Hua-yen's doctrine of mutual interpenetration with Whitehead's organic philosophy.[35] But the parallel breaks down with regard to the symmetrical inclusion of past and future in each other. The first of the "ten mysteries" of Hua-yen is "the mystery of simultaneous completion and mutual correspondence." Chang says of this principle that it

> implies not only the Non-Obstruction of space and time but more significantly, it implies the simultaneous existence of all causes and effects. In the dimension of Shih-shih Wu-ai all causes and effects, regardless of kind or of realm, must be simultaneously established without hindrance of omission. Should we consider this to be a form of absolute determinism? From men's viewpoint, this certainly appears to be the case. How can effects in the future be brought into the past without first being determined? Here again we encounter the familiar Svabhāva way of thinking: determinativeness precedes all entities and events.[36]

Francis H. Cook, who also notes the parallel between Hua-yen and Whitehead, stresses Fa-tsang's use of the part-whole construction to interpret interpenetration.[37] Just as a rafter is not a rafter except insofar as it is in place in a building, so the building is not what it is except insofar as it has that rafter. Now the part-whole model is not necessarily expressive of the temporal dimension, being a spatial form. But Cook courageously draws out its temporal implications in his discussion of the Bodhisattva. If a Bodhisattva at any stage already contains the later stages, what is the point of effort and vows? He quotes Fa-tsang:

> If one stage is acquired, all stages are acquired, because (each stage) possesses the six characteristics (of universality and particularity, etc.), because of the infinite interrelationship of primary and secondary, because of mutual interpenetration, because of mutual identity, and because of mutual interfusion. The *Avataṁsaka Sūtra* says, "One stage includes the qualities of all stages throughout." Therefore, what is meant here is the acquisition of all stages as well as the stage of Buddhahood as soon as one has reached that part (of the path) which is called "superior progress," which is the perfection of faith. Because all stages including the stage of

Buddhahood are identical, then cause and effect are not different, and beginning and end interpenetrate. On each stage, one is both a Bodhisattva and a Buddha.[38]

Cook's answer to that question is a somewhat thin expression of the commitment to complete the path and to live *as if* one were already the Buddha.[39]

As Hartshorne and others have argued, human action, even that of a Bodhisattva, is morally significant and responsible only if the results of the action depend in part on a choice that could have been made another way. Furthermore, as Hartshorne points out, Buddhism and Whitehead agree in their recognition of the base of moral motivation as the identity of any future outcomes with oneself, undercutting all egoistic theories which might claim that some outcomes are in one's self-interest.[40] Compassion is a metaphysical truth, not merely a psychological achievement. Essential to this view of responsibility and compassion is the recognition of asymmetry in the causal, temporal process. As we noted in the previous section, Nāgārjuna did not refute the conception that nature involves asymmetrical causal procession, and we may note now that, at least within the moral sphere, one ought to hold to such a view of asymmetry.

But then in a very crucial sense, we should not say that past and future interpenetrate, that the future is fully determinate in the past. Put another way, from the standpoint of our present activity, there are some relations that will come to be in the future that are not determined now; because of this, responsibility for the future rests partly in our own activity and cannot be traced back to infinitely remote prior causes as in an everlasting and reversible billiard game. Process philosophy has helped to articulate the importance of non-determinism in causality.[41]

This suggests that it is a mistake for Buddhism, ala Altizer or Hua-yen to interpret interpenetration or interrelation as entailing the symmetry of earlier and later times. But perhaps Buddhism need not interpret causality this way. Fa-tsang said (italics added):

The mystery of simultaneous completeness means that all the above mentioned ten principles simultaneously establish themselves in correspondence, to form a (totalistic) dependent-arising, without the differentiation of past or future, beginning or end. In this dimension, all and all establish themselves in perfect consistency and freedom. This establishment of totalistic dependent-arising makes all things and principles mutually penetrate into one another, *yet does not upset their orders in any individual realm.*[42]

What Fa-tsang should mean by this, I believe, (whatever he in fact meant) is that within the causal realm of process, particularly moral process, there exists whatever indeterminacy and asymmetry as would be found in an ordinary analysis, *and that the mutual penetration is to be understood on a different level.* I shall present a theory that expresses this distinction.[43]

Anything which has an identity—any occasion, any eternal object, any *dharma*—is determinate. To be determinate is for a thing to be itself in relation to at least one other thing, to be determinate "in respect to" something. To have an identity, therefore, is to be a complexity of two kinds of features, conditional features and essential features. Conditional features are those a thing has by virtue of the things with respect to which it is determinate. Essential features are those it has intrinsic to itself by virtue of which it can stand in relation to what conditions it. Without essential features a thing could not be different from other things and, therefore, could not relate to them as being conditioned. Without conditional features a thing could not be determinate with respect to anything.

A thing is a *de facto* harmony of essential and conditional features. This statement has two aspects. The first is that the thing would not be determinate at all without both. Without essential features, the conditional features would not be different from the set of other things with respect to which the thing is supposed to be determinate. Without conditional features, the essential features would not be determinately different from anything else, and hence not determinate at all. So determinateness itself, the very being of determinate being, requires the *de facto* harmony of both kinds of features.

The second aspect is that the harmony is called *de facto* because it cannot be grounded in either the conditional features or the essential features, and the harmony of both together is a condition for both. The conditional features, which are what we often refer to as the external causes (although the Buddhists are right that "conditioning causes" include far more than "efficient causes"), contribute to the harmony but do not "account" for it because they do not cause the essential features. With the conditional features alone there would be no new determinate thing, only the things with respect to which it would be determinate if it were determinate. The essential features do not account for the harmony because they are indeterminate except insofar as they are already harmonized with the conditional features. They presuppose their togetherness with conditional features, and therefore cannot account for it. Lacking all "account," the *de facto* harmonies are "empty" in the profoundest ontological sense. Emptiness does not consist in the fact that each thing reduces completely to its conditional features, and therefore, to the things which condition it (this is a common but erroneous interpretation of *pratītya-samutpāda*). Nor does emptiness consist in the identification of a thing with its essential features which are indeterminate and thus mystically merged with the essential features of all things. The first interpretation of emptiness leads to nihilism and the second to mystical eternalism. The Middle Way is to acknowledge that emptiness consists in the *de facto* harmony of essential and conditional features.

These distinctions can be illustrated with the conceptions of process philosophy. An occasion is a *de facto* harmony of antecedent occasion prehended and those features determining the subjective form by which the prehensions are integrated. The occasions prehended are the conditional features, although how they condition the occasion depends upon how they are determined to fit together in the emerging subject. The essential features that can determine that fit may be of three kinds. Essential features stemming from the past are past occasions prehended objectively which also function to determine the emerging subjective form; continuity of an individual through time, for instance, expresses some of these reiterating essential features. Essential features stemming from the future are those determining obligation and what Whitehead called the superjective character of the process of integration. Most interesting, however, are the essential features stemming from the immediate moment of coming to be; they are spontaneous relative to what the past entails, and creative of whatever new realities of integration come to be that allow the new occasion to emerge. The subjective immediacy of coming to be is the reality of, and sometimes the awareness of, the emerging *de facto* harmony of essential and conditional features.

A further distinction may now be drawn that is crucial for rendering the Buddhist sense of interrelationship. The character a thing has, and all the relations involved in that character, may be called cosmological. This includes both essential and conditional features, and all the causal and other determinate ways things are related to one another. But *that* a thing is, with whatever cosmological nature it has, is ontological. A thing can be understood in both cosmological and ontological dimensions. Understanding *what* it is, is cosmological; understanding *that* it is, is ontological.

From a cosmological perspective, as a *de facto* harmony a thing is empty. The same characteristic viewed ontologically, however, reveals something different, namely that to be at all, things must be in an ontological context of mutual relevance deeper than their cosmological, relative conditioning. The proof for this is as follows. Consider two things each of which has conditional features relative to the other. The cosmological relations between them are limited to those conditional features, for instance how one limits the other. The cosmological relations make possible the determinate relations between the two *de facto* harmonies; but for there to be the cosmological relations, the conditional features must be determinate, which is possible only in harmony with the essential features. Therefore, for the cosmological relations to be possible there must be an ontologically enabling context in which the two things with their essential features are mutually together. The ontological context of mutual relevance is a togetherness of determining things more basic than their conditional relations, because it involves a togetherness of their essential features too. For one thing to be determinate as a harmony of essential features, it must be together with other things, not only conditionally but with regard to essential features.

The Buddhist aesthetic vision of the interrelationship of things in their immediate factual character is, I submit, an appreciation of the ontological context of mutual relevance. It is a basic ontological vision of what it is to be determinate, a *dharma*. And it is compatible with any kinds of cosmological relations we might find to exist, because all cosmological relations are matters of conditional features. Consider, for instance, whether a future state of affairs is completely determined in an antecedent state. If it is (the doctrine of causal symmetry), then the later and earlier states have *de facto* harmonies entirely determined by their conditional features relative to each other, or at least, the essential features of the later make no objective difference. On the other hand, if the causal process is asymmetrical, then there are some important essential features in the later events that do not derive from the earlier ones.

If there are independent cosmological reasons for preferring an assymetrical, non-deterministic account of process, then this is perfectly compatible with the deeper ontological interrelatedness or interpenetration that consists in the ontological context of mutual relevance. In the case of indeterminism, the later event would not be able to have those novelty-producing essential features that make it different from the antecedent event if the earlier and later events were not ontologically together in a context of mutual relevant. If they were not in that context, then the novelty-producing, essential features would be indeterminate, and hence incapable, in fact, of producing novelty.

Review

The metaphors of whole versus part, and of all-time-together versus a finite time, are both cosmological metaphors, taking their force from conditional features of spatial and temporal relation. The abstract categories defining "ontological context of mutual relevance" can indicate that the religious vision grasps a genuinely ontological interrelatedness, not cosmological connections.

There is an even greater religious depth to the ontological dimension. The phrase "ontological context of mutual relevance" connotes the passivity of being a presupposition. To grasp or envision the ontological dimension, however, is to become aware of the immediacy of reality. Without that ontological context, there would be nothing, no *de facto* harmonies, no conditional features, no essential features, no *dharmas* at all. The immediate facticity of things, their dappled presence, their shining forth, suggests what has in the West been construed as divine creativity. Of course, it has been common to construe divine creativity cosmologically. That is, God is interpreted as one entity causing others, often in a temporal sense. But if God is a determinate causal entity, then God must be in an ontological context of mutual relevance with the world, and that ontological context would be more "creative" than God. Whitehead saw that God interpreted as a cosmological actual entity must be different from the creativity that underlies the prehensive relations between God and the world.[44]

Divine creativity need not be interpreted cosmologically, however. The mystical tradition and, in their most reflective moments, many of the great Western theologians have interpreted creativity ontologically. That is, the "presence" of God in the world is the world's own "acts of existence." But precisely because the ontological possibility of things requires that they be in an ontological context of mutual relevance, the creative act by which things are is "unified." The unity is not in the cosmological characters of the created things, for the creative spontaneity of some things is over here rather than over there and at this time rather than some other time. Rather, the unity is at the level of the ontological context of mutual relevance. Within Whitehead's conceptuality, for instance, the immediate creative spontaneity of an occasion must combine with the occasions it prehends, and each of those occasions is a combination of their own spontaneities with what they in turn had previously prehended, and so on. So whereas the dates and places of the creative manifestations are diverse, the connection in the ontological context of mutual relevance is unified; otherwise, the creativity would not ground the *de facto* harmonies of things whose essential features are cosmologically disjunctive.

The ontological function of divine creativity, as appreciated in yogic awareness or enlightenment, stands in an advanced relation to both Buddhism and Western thought. Since there is no divine creator who determinately transcends the *de facto*, empty, created *dharmas,* it is true to say, on the theory proposed, that *nirvāṇa* is *saṃsāra.* But the theory rejects any attempts to render the underlying unity of the world in a cosmological way, to deny differences, to say that the absolute unity is real and the phenomenal diversity is extrinsically caused, as in the common water-wave metaphor; differences are precisely what is created. Yet the unity of the creative act constituting the ontological context of mutual relevance is not to be reduced to the cosmological plurality of the thises and thats.

On the theory proposed, the appeal to creativity is not an attempt to explain things by a determinate principle of creativity; as determinate, any principle would have to be among the things explained. Rather, it is an appeal to what, for want of a better term, can be called a creative or decisive action; to know that is not to grasp a principle, but to locate and respond in wonder to an act. Buddhistic enlightenment very well captures the empirical sense of *finding* the ontological ground, not grasping it rationally.

With respect to Western thought it is plausible to interpret divine creativity as God. Of course, insofar as "God" is supposed to be a determinate entity who has a character apart from the product of creative exericse, it is incompatible with this theory which is then atheistic. But there are many precedents within the West for construing God as determinate only in the world, and as indeterminate apart from the world. Since names are bestowed and not claimed, it is best to leave it to others to label this theory.

My conclusion is simply to note that the service process philosophy can perform for Buddhism is to force it to a recognition of the difference between cosmology and ontology, and to abandon its sometimes too-cute attack on speculative thinking when it means to be attacking only a cosmological rendition of religion. Whitehead has provided, even with various modifications, a theory that adequately articulates the Buddhist insights regarding process and causation, its doctrine of *pratītya-samutpāda.* What Buddhism can do for process philosophy is not only to provide it with allies in its repunctuating of the history of the West it can also call it to abandon the inadequate conceptions of God as distinct from creativity, and to develop a more profound ontology. For thinkers who are not concerned to "represent" positions, East or West, the encounter of Buddhism with process philosophy has already made a creative advance beyond what each originally brought to the encounter. This is a Middle Way between the eternalistic theory that "all is one," which mistakenly denies the truth of event pluralism in process, and the nihilism of the modern West, which noting the death of the cosmological God, concludes that nothing is holy.

Prefatory Remarks to Hajime Nakamura's Essay

One of the leading Japanese thinkers presents a succinct yet profound accounting of man's nexus of existence. Nakamura returns to the Buddhist doctrine of interrelational origination (pratītya-samutpāda) *to develop a consistent theory of existence, i.e., that no man lives independently or in absolute isolation. He gives telling examples to delineate the fact of dissimilarity in all existences, that no twins may claim exactitude or identity, however similar they seem to be. Each has a biological history, to be sure, but each also has traits that surpass mere empirical descriptions. The differences inevitably show up and we are at a loss at how to cope with such differences, but Nakamura shows the way to understanding them in terms of interrelational origination.*

Western thinkers from the early Greeks, such as Plato and Aristotle, and modern thinkers, such as Descartes, Leibniz and Kant, were unable to satisfactorily grapple with the concepts of identity, change and continuity in human existence until the recent rise of modern physics. This earlier metaphysics was basically non-pragmatic, speculative and substance-oriented. It showed how things happen but not why. The East, on the other hand, saw man's nature, not aloof with towering principles geared for descriptive purposes, but inviolably bonded in the very dynamics of man's contingent interrelationship. It simply tells us why things happen and thereby points the way to mastering and controlling human relationship.

9

Interrelational Existence

Hajime Nakamura

Man is a social creature. To communicate with others, he needs information, but the information and communication take on unique features. For example, we say that a man maintains his own individuality, his unique existence; he is different from other individuals in terms of character, nature and existence. He has a perspective which singles him out from any other person. In other words, to know that a man is living does not mean that he is living in the same way as others do or that he can be treated likewise. His intrinsic personality exhibits the fact that he is what he is because he implicates other persons as well as many other things in his experiences.

Livelihood, in short, requires all kinds of relationship. Consider, for instance, the fact that the basic needs of man, food, shelter and clothing, involve countless number of people in multifarious relational chain and function. Each of the basic needs shows up the vast and social network in which man participates in terms of being a provider as well as a consumer. The relatedness of existence penetrates so deeply that it is difficult to isolate any one person or one thing in the total existential sphere. This is the reason why in Japanese the term for human being is *ningen* which literally means "between or among men." The relational nature of man qua man is so basic, so thoroughly accepted as a premise, that only in acknowledgement of it can there be intercourse and communication. Given such definition and understanding of the concept of man or human being, it is meaningless to speak of an independently existing person or to discuss a subject without its total nexus. Philosophers may fall into some form of solipsism by focusing on and accepting the subject and its functions. But for one who lives in the total social context, the nature and functions of a subject are mere play of words or ideas.

Is there such a phenomenon as a lonely man in an isolated place? Is he really isolated from others and the surroundings? An example of a Japanese ex-soldier who lived on Wake Island for 30 years after the end of hostilities may be introduced. The question is, Was he really alone? Was he really living in a vacuum? All accounts indicate that he was far from being alone and isolated. He was constantly using tools, doing things he had learned, and he was forever improvising in order to sustain himself. Although the isolation was forced upon him by his respect for the governmental orders he had received as a soldier, the fact remains that he kept on living in relationship to his superiors and his immediate commitments. In essence, he lived among the people, real or imagined, and therefore was not alone at all.

Biological life also proves that an individual in total isolation is not possible. One is either a male or female at birth and one continues to live and support the biological chain. The genealogy of a male or female can be traced into the remote past, but the point is that the present state of being is the result of huge ancestral influences, a transmission that has taken on very subtle but sure measures over a long period of time. Thus the so-called chain of biological traits is an established fact for every person. The genealogical past gives one a sense of certainty or the determined nature of things, but there is no guarantee of certainty with respect to the future since it requires or depends on various conditions over which we have no absolute control.

It is a simple fact that individuals have need for the opposite sex. Such individuals affirm the fact that there are biological as well as other types of relationship at all times. An individual without any relationship is a fiction, an abstraction. It simply does not obtain. In consequence, the continuity of life by the male and female biological relationship exhibits an important basis for the signification of what we call humankind.

Biological traits may be transferred to the offspring but it is not the case with cultural traits. For example, the traits of an established family occupation or profession cannot be transmitted. An individual does not create things alone. He requires the cooperation and presence of other persons and things to foster the idea—surroundings in which something arises. A number of people is involved in furnishing the proper ambience for something to happen. In fact, there are certain things that the single individual cannot do by himself simply because the isolation and independency that he desires are not forthcoming as he is already bound to interrelational existence.

In our society, we witness an anomaly in regard to legal matters. That is to say, laws assume that man is independent or that he can be treated as an isolated case. But, as we are aware, such a premise postulated by law is not true at all. It is a mere assumption which cannot support the absolute status of the individual. In consequence, it can be asserted that laws in general are not true reflectiors of man's existence or of his nature.

Individuality is another puzzling term. As we focus on or examine the nature of individuality, we find that the whole social matrix is not observed, because the individuality will take precedence over the whole. But the concept of individuality is an abstraction, even though it persists. Why is this? How does the nature and concept of individuality arise? Or, in what way can we speak of the individual? We must pursue these questions.

We casually speak of a life of one's own in the sense that an individual life can be lived through the absolute terms. But can this be proven? That is, can it be proved that one's existence is solely one's own, that it can be distinguished clearly in no unmistakable terms from other individuals or persons? One certainly would be hard put to justify such a position. There are physical differences due to the makeup of various genes, to be sure, but to prove that self A is altogether different from self B in terms of individuality is suspect. In this connection, the Cartesian self or ego is difficult to uphold or maintain. Its weakness is in looking for or at an independently existing self, an entity that cannot be found anywhere. The fallacy here is that we tend to think about a self in substantial terms, i.e., as a substance, as something entirely alone and different from another substance.

A typical example of the substantial treatment of the self is found in Leibniz's system of monads or monadology. His philosophy is a form of monism where the concept of individuality is taken to be absolute. In the past we have seen philosophies where the monistic absolute failed to present us with true answers as to the concept of individuality, as in Hegel, Spinoza, Vedānta and even Marx. All monistic systems, whether of the microscopic or macroscopic scale, have so-called built-in problems. Let us pursue the problem with respect to Leibniz.

Leibniz asserted that there are an infinite number of monads. Each monad is a simple, indivisible substance. There are no parts and this means that a monad cannot have an expansive feature. Each is a substance whose nature lies at the bottom of the whole universe—everything is made up of these monads. He speaks of monads as perceptions, not in the strictly conscious sense, but in terms of general psychological perceptions in what he labels "petite perceptions." In terms of perceptions, each monad is independent of each other's perception. There is power of perception in each and this is what gives it its own individuality, such perception, however, being mere reflection of other monads. This phenomenon is possible because each monad is windowless. It is here that Leibniz has gone as far as he could on his monadology.

Leibniz fails to explain why each monad is different or unique, although he asserts that each one is uniquely different from any other. There is no basis upon which each monad can be said to be different. In nature, as we well know, there are no two identical entities. Leibniz seems to work in this vein, but fails to prove the nature of identity and difference in terms of the growth and development of monads.

A further question arises here: If the monads are windowless, how could they interact with each other and thereby develop different individualities? What brings the interaction about? So long as Leibniz adheres to the substance context of monads, he will not be able to explain adequately the individual differences or how different characteristics exist in individual forms.

In order to explain the true nature of differences in individual existences, aspects, forms and appearances, we must be able to accept or subscribe to a different context, a framework in which every individual, so to speak, receives influences from other individuals as well as from all other things. The influence or influencing forces exist in different degrees in other individuals and things. Thus each individual receives influences from the world at large, each having different receptions and thereby developing in a different manner, although the world seemingly remains the same. Thus, the Leibnizian explanation of differences in monads also fails to account for the relational nature of the monads themselves. In this respect, Kantian philosophy also faces the same problem. Kant talks about different personalities, but basically he does this in the abstract. He gives a model of perception, but fails to adequately explain how or why there are differences in perceptions by individuals with respect to colors, tones, tastes, etc. For this reason, it can be concluded that there is a limitation to Kantian epistemology.

Let us take the case of a set of identical twins, of the same sex, either male or female, and let us call them A and B. A will be given training in the aesthetic area, in cultural pursuits and perceptions. B, on the other hand, will be given training in the physical area, in gymnastics and strong sturdy types of work. Both will grow up in ways that anyone could spot the differences between A and B. Should they be brought up in different countries the differences between them will be even more dramatic in terms of preferences in food, clothing, etc., and even in spoken language. All of this must be attributed to countless conditions and causes imposed by an immeasurable past that brings forth unique personalities. Considered in this light, we must admit that all things in the universe do contribute toward the formation of such personalities.

In Buddhism, the "causes" and "conditions" are referred to in Sanskrit as *kāraṇa-hetu* (efficient cause) and *adhipateya* or *adhipati-pratyaya* (dominant condition). They govern the way certain experiences arise or manifest. In Japenese, these causal conditions are referred to as *innen*, where the *in* delineates the internal causal nature and *nen* the external conditional or relational nature, thus depicting the total way in which influences are taking place. Such a thorough way to describe the causal nature of things was not seen in the ancient West. Aristotle, it will be recalled, spoke of the four causes, namely, material, efficient, formal and final, but this did not go far enough into the nature of internal and external relations. His philosophy was essentially bound up in the substance-view of all happenings. Vedānta philosophy in ancient India did not fare better since it was oriented toward the metaphysically absolute and neutral Brahman.

In jurisprudence of the West, there is a phrase, *causa sine qua non* (an indispensable cause or condition). This notion has some similarity to the Japanese *innen* whereby everything is included. Yet in the West, the notion of cause or condition is still tinged heavily with the nature of mere relationship of entities. In some ways, modern science subscribes to the Buddhist way of causation; both have common grounds, but it has to be said that Buddhism really has nothing to do with science per se. Where science is limited to the perceived world of objects, Buddhism goes beyond those objects to the network of causes which range into the non-perceived world. In this sense, Buddhism goes into the depths of existence.

In the Buddhist framework of causal nexus, we are able to explain the uniqueness of personalities by way of the internal causes from the past and the external relational conditions of the present happenings. No two causes or conditions are identical and, therefore, there are no identical happenings ever. Thus, in the case of identical twins, no set is identical in a nondistinguishable sense. There will always be differences, however subtle and indistinguishable they are alleged to be. Each is uniquely different by virtue of the casual conditions received from its seemingly infinite past experiences. In Japanese Buddhism, this indebtedness to the past is called *on* and it means more specifically that we are all that we are in virtue of being nurtured by all conditions of the world, past and present.

In the realm of physical experiences, persons will be treated with certain fixed numbers and features. Thus, there is a sense of determinism and control over those persons. We speak for example, of a unit of people, i.e., a set number, in government or a business enterprise. Such reference to a group of people, however, does not reveal the whole causal nature of the persons concerned. For, afterall, there is the non-fixed, non-determined, nature relative to those persons. Each person has a unique past which others are not able to match or duplicate; each has his own birthdate, place of birth, parentage, friends, relatives, etc. all of which mark him off as an incomparable personality and he will continue to distinguish himself in his own way.

Consequently, it is important to acknowledge the debt owed to unseen causal forces at play from the distant past and to assert one's existence in no uncertain terms. At that moment one may utter: "I alone exist incomparably" *(yuiga dokuson)*. This is not an utterance of self-conceit, but a very humble Buddhist way of showing gratitude for one's life that has causal and conditional relations from a remote past.

The causal and conditional principle applies equally to the future. For example, take two persons, A and B. Both will have their respective unique roles to play in the visible domain, which can be measured and manipulated to a large extent. But in the deepest sense, each person must be seen as performing his role in the total framework, i.e., the causal and conditional natures that stem from the past to the present and that will continue into the future. And only in this sense can we speak of individuals A and B as being valuable and precious relative to their roles, and in fact, this is the way they are respected and dignified. In everyday life, we see abundant examples where individuals are accounted for only in terms of the visible features or characteristics—the amount of money amassed or the level of success one has achieved. Such matters are measurable quantities and do not reveal the total personality. But as an individual is unique in unmeasurable ways, he is also irreplaceable in the invisible sense. In consequence, we may consider the nature of a self as having two aspects: (a) the visible and measurable aspect and (b) the invisible and unmeasurable aspect.

To expand on this, take a person who is a millionaire, 6 feet tall and weighs 200 pounds. He is, as we normally say, a man whose assets can be measured or calculated. He even has a social status which can be measured and thus becomes another asset. But the question here is, Is that all with respect to this man? From our discussion, it is to be noted that he also has unmeasurable qualities which come into play from his internal, invisible forces and establish him in his meaningful livelihood. In short, the measurable quantities must be combined with the unmeasurable qualities to present us with a complete picture of the man. The important point here is to acknowledge the fact that even a small man, or a man of any size for that matter, can perfect himself or his unique personality, despite the presence of overbearing outward or external manifestation. He can become great in that respect.

Man then lives in terms of the total or entire universe of things. Each individual is a mirror that reflects that universe. Each is a small universe in his own right. It must be emphasized, however, that this little universe is always unique and irreplaceable. When such realization comes about, i.e., the identity of the uniqueness of the small and extensive universe, there is the grasp of the essence of the entirety, the holistic nature of things. In short, there is a correspondence of the small and great universes. Thus as one takes an action, it cannot be an isolated case or separated from the rest of the universe; it is involved in the numerous conditions that prevail in the universe. When an insight is arrived at in terms of this holistic condition, we may say that truth has been attained with regard to one's own ability or power. A Buddhist sutra says:

> Adjusting or manipulating the laws of the universe to suit one's own conduct expresses the state of mere ordinary existence. However, correcting oneself in accordance with the laws of the universe is the attainment of Buddhahood. The realization of this principle of life is the achievement of enlightenment.

In expressing themselves, the Japanese Jōdo Shinshū (True Pure Land) Buddhist Sect followers humbly say: "I am permitted to do this or that," rather than, "I do this or that." The underlying thought here is, of course, that one cannot do anything by oneself, but instead one is able to do things owing to the aid and help offered by many people and conditions. In the same sect, one of the basic thoughts is expressed as "the Buddha gave me the faith," just as in Christianity it is said that one is "saved by the grace of God." In both cases, it would seem that the Buddha and God are set up in opposition to oneself, as an object of worship. Looked upon from the standpoint of the totality of the universe, however, the opposition no longer remains, for the entire universe corresponds to the very existence of the individual. In consequence, the concept of enlightenment in Buddhism is not such a far-fetched thing that one could treat it lightly or ridicule it as nonsensical and meaningless in our lives.

Enlightenment is an achievable reality, especially in terms of what we have delineated in the nature of man who is in total relationship within the vast universe.

The concept of equality is another misunderstood term. In any real society, it is never completely in force. Even in communist countries, equality is advertised or spoken of with great enthusiasm, but in actuality, due to severe class consciousness, the inequality is even more sharp and prominent. Equality in communist countries is actually a myth, a dream, that does not relate to the real situation. Political realities are too overbearing and oppressive for justice to prevail. Yet we must not lose sight of the basic fact that all persons of whatever persuasion are and can be equal as individuals.

The equality of a person does not come by merely by associating with other persons, earning a living, or maintaining one's individuality. It comes, on the other hand, by a person who, as a small universe, reflects the entire universe of existence. It reveals, as mentioned earlier, an inclusive nature in terms of the visible as well as invisible spheres of existence. When the proper relationship or link is made by the person, there will come to him the quality of dignity and respect, a recognition that he is not merely a conglomeration of external manifestation, but a being rooted deeply in his total conditional past.

The dignity of human beings is spoken of quite casually nowadays, but there is a bit of hypocrisy in it because, in real society, humans are treated as a fixed lot, as a unit. There is no dignified treatment in this. But there is, on the other hand, a real sense of being a person, that others are also real persons, and that the perception of this quality issues forth in sympathetic relationship with others and will bring forth a sense of joy in living. It is the unique feeling of sharing with others the common elements of being within the infinite and immeasurable sphere of existence, a true feeling of embracing everyone from the bottom of the heart,, which is but another way of expressing the depths of universal interrelational existence.

We started this essay with the notion of communication. We stated that the information communicated takes on unique features. We hope we have adequately analyzed the significant factors involved in exchanging information and, indeed, understanding the true nature of person-to-person exchanges. Communication need not remain on the external level, in the social, physiological or physical spheres, but more importantly, it should reach into the depths of beings so that people may realize and share the concerns, joys and happiness of one another. Rightly understood and employed, communication is the resolution of the dichotomy in man and the revelation of things as they are in their truly interpenetrative nature.

Notes

Introduction: The Buddhist-American Encounter in Philosophy

1. Donald Lach, *Asia in the Making of Europe* (Chicago: University of Chicago Press, 1965), vol. I, xx.

2. Alfred North Whitehead, *Process and Reality* (New York: The Free Press, 1978), 7.

3. Kenneth K. Inada, "Whitehead's 'actual entity' and the Buddha's *anātman*," *Philosophy East and West*, vol. XXI (July 1971), 303.

4. Venkata Ramanan, *Nāgārjuna's Philosophy: As Presented in the Mahā-Prajñāpāramitā-Śāstra* (Toyko: Charles E. Tuttle, Co., Inc., 1966), 248. *Cf.* Bhikkhu Ñanānanda, *Concept and Reality in Early Buddhist Thought* (Kandy: Buddhist Publication Society, 1971), 39ff.

5. Alfred North Whitehead, *Modes of Thought* (New York: The Free Press, 1966), 151.

6. F.S.C. Northrop, "Forword," in D.W. Sherburne, *A Whiteheadian Aesthetic* (New Haven: Yale University Press, 1961), xxv.

7. Kenneth K. Inada, *Nāgārjuna: A Translation of His Mūlamadhyamak-akārikā* (Toyko: The Hokuseido Press, 1970, 1975), 39.

8. Guy Richard Welbon, *The Buddhist Nirvāṇa and its Western Interpreters* (Chicago: University of Chicago Press, 1968), 304.

9. Herbert Guenther, *Philosophy and Psychology in the Abhidharma* (Berkeley: Shambhala, 1974), 241.

10. John M. Koller, *Oriental Philosophies* (New York: Charles Scribner's Sons, 1970), 193.

11. Lama Anagarika Govinda, *The Psychological Attitude of Early Buddhist Philosophy* (London: Rider & Co., 1961), 57.

12. *The Philosophy of Alfred North Whitehead*, ed. P. A. Schilpp (New York: Library of Living Philosophers, Tudor Publishing Co., 1941, 1951), 489.

13. Gordon Allport, *Becoming* (New Haven: Yale University Press, 1955), 51.

14. Alfred North Whitehead, *Religion in the Making* (Cleveland: World Publishing Co., 1926), 87.

15. Marjorie Grene, *The Knower and the Known* (New York: Basic Books inc., 1966), 224, 251f.

16. Nolan Pliny Jacobson, *Buddhism: The religion of Analysis* (Carbondale: Southern Illinois University Press, 1970, 1974, 1979), Chaps. 4, 5.

2. David L. Hall, *The Width of Civilized Experience: Comparative Philosophy and the Pursuit of Excellence*

1. For a detailed discussion of the principal reasons for the dominance of the moral and scientific interests in our culture see my book, *The Uncertain Phoenix*, (New York: Fordham University Press 1981), passim.

2. *Science and Civilization in China*, vol. 2 (Cambridge: Cambridge University Press, 1962), Section 18, 579.

3. *Science and the Modern World* (New York: Free Press, 1967), 208.

4. Ibid., 152.

5. One should precisely *not* look to *The Poetics* for an appreciation of the aesthetic sensibility. Apart from a brief, brilliant paragraph on metaphor in Chapter 22, one could well read Aristotle's treatment of artistic production as an extension of his *Ethics* and *Politics*.

6. I am, of course, aware that certain developments in contemporary science, particularly in micro-physics, call for a renewed emphasis upon aesthetic and mystical understandings. It is significant that those promoting such an emphasis find themselves drawn inevitably to oriental thought. For a popular account of this as yet minority movement see Fritjof Capra's *The Tao of Physics* (Berkeley: Shambhala Press, 1975). Also, see the interesting recent article in *Philosophy East and West*, "In Defense of Mystical Science," vol. 29, No. 1 (January, 1979): 73–90.

7. (New York: Harper and Row, 1972).

8. If we were to seek a parallel for this kind of art in the West, we could perhaps locate it in certain painters of the later Middle Ages, such as Giotto or Fra Fillipo Lippi. See Jeanne L. Trabold, "The Influence of Chinese Painting on European Art of the Late Middle Ages and Early Renaissance: An Hypothesis," *Selected Papers in Asian Studies* (Albuquerque, New Mexico: Western Conference of the Association for Asian Studies, 1976): 53–59.

9. Translated and quoted by Chung-Yuan Chang, *Creativity and Taoism* (N.Y.: Harper & Row Publishers, Inc., 1970 edition), 57.

10. I hope I shall be forgiven the use of this barbarism which combines a Latin and a Greek root in order to explicate what is, predominently, a Buddhist insight! For a complete discussion of these types of mystical sense see "The Way Beyond 'Ways,'" Chap. 5, in *The Uncertain Phoenix*.

11. This illustration is given in some detail in Garma C. C. Chang's *The Buddhist Teaching of Totality* (University Park: The Pennsylvania State University Press, 1974), 22–24. The Hall of Mirrors is an alternative version of the doctrine

of Indra's Net, which consists of an intricately interwoven network of crystal ornaments hung above the Heavens. The network reflects the entire universe and each crystal reflects all images, no detail being lost.

12. And even that inference is a questionable one. See *Religion in the Making* (New York: Meridian Books, Inc., 1971), 69.

13. See Donald Sherburne, "Whitehead Without God," in Delwin Brown, *et al.*; eds., *Process Philosophy and Christian Thought* (New York: Bobbs-Merrill, 1972), 305–28.

14. See *Process and Reality* (New York: Macmillan, 1929), 370–71.

15. *Religion in the Making*, 55.

16. Ibid., 50.

17. *Process and Reality*, 517.

18. *Modes of Thought* (New York: The Free Press, 1968), 120.

19. *Religion in the Making*, 16.

20. There is a certain tendentiousness in the Arguments of this essay, perhaps suggestive of a reverse cultural chauvinism, in that I have argued for the resort to Oriental modes of thought without stressing the obvious fact that it would likely be profitable, for example, for Buddhists to seek out the cultural evidences of Anglo-European thought. For just as there is a weakness in our understanding based upon too great an emphasis upon moral and scientific evidences, there is, perhaps, an analogous defect in Oriental thought due to an over emphasizing of aesthetic and mystical sensibilities.

3. Nolan Pliny Jacobson, *A Buddhist Analysis of Human Experience*

1. Alfred North Whitehead, "An Address to Boys in England," in *Science and Philosophy* (Paterson, N.J.: New Student Outline Series, Littlefield, Adams & Co., 1964 ed.): 174.

2. Edward T. Hall, *Beyond Culture* (Garden City, N.Y.: Doubleday & Co., Inc., Anchor Books Edition, 1977), 240.

3. Joseph Needham, *Science and Civilization in China* (London: Cambridge University Press, 1954), vol. 1: 9.

4. Lewis Thomas, review of *Hiroshima and Nagasaki: The Physical, Medical and Social Effects of the Atomic Bombings*, by the Committee for the Compilation of Materials on Damage Caused by the Atomic Bombs in Hiroshima and Nagasaki, trans. Eisei Ishikawa and David L. Swain (New York: Basic Books, 1981); and of *Unforgettable Fire: Pictures Drawn by Atomic Bomb Survivors*, ed. Japan Broadcasting Corp. (New York: Pantheon, 1981), *The New York Review*, (September 24, 1981): 3.

5. F. S. C. Northrop, *The Meeting of East and West* (New York: Macmillan Co., 1946), 399.

6. John Dewey, "Qualitative Thought," in *Representative Selections from Dewey on Experience Nature and Freedom* Richard J. Bernstein ed. (Indianapolis: The Bobbs-Merrill Co., Inc., 1960): 185.

7. Ibid., 176.

8. John J. McDermott, *The Culture of Experience* (New York: New York University Press, 1976), ix.

9. Kitarō Nishida, "Affective Feeling," in *Japanese Phenomenology: Philosophy as a Transcultural Approach*, eds. Yoshihiro Nitta, Eiichi Shimomisse and Hirotaka Tatematsu (Dordrecht, Holland: D. Reidel Publishing Co., 1979): 66–67.

10. Ibid., 226.

11. Ibid., 246, 264.

12. Nolan Pliny Jacobson, *Buddhism and the Contemporary World: Change and Self-Correction* (Carbondale: Southern Illinois Univdersity Press, 1983), chap. 4.

13. *Collected Papers of Charles Sanders Peirce* ed. Arthur W. Burks, vol. 2, par. 536, (Cambridge: Harvard University Press, 1958). Henceforth referred to as CPP.

14. Charles Hartshorne, *Creative Synthesis and Philosophic Method* (LaSalle, Ill.: The Open Court Publishing Co., 1970), 76.

15. Alfred North Whitehead, *Process and Reality* (New York: The Free Press, 1978), 18.

16. CPP, eds. Charles Hartshorne and Paul Weiss, vol. 1, par. 357, 1934.

17. CPP, vol. 6, par. 553, ibid.

18. Charles Hartshorne, *Whitehead's Philosophy: Selected Essays, 1935–1970* (Lincoln, Nebr.: University of Nebraska Press, 1972), 131.

19. See Kenneth K. Inada, "Whitehead's 'Actual Entity' and the Buddha's *anātman*," *Philosophy East and West*, vol. 21 (July 1971): 303.

20. Alfred North Whitehead, *Religion in the Making* (New York: The Macmillan Co., 1926), 119.

21. Ibid., 147.

22. Whitehead, *Science and Philosophy*, pp. 225, 226, 235. (Originally published as "Harvard: The Future," *Atlantic Monthly*, Sept. 1936). (Italics added).

23. By the West, or Western civilization, I mean those nations that have been shaped by classical Greek philosophy and drama, Roman law, Catholic Christianity (as distinct from the Eastern Orthodox Church), the Reformation, the Renaissance, the American and French Revolutions, and the Age of Science and Technology.

24. Robert N. Bellah, *Beyond Belief* (New York: Harper & Row, 1970). See also his essay, "The Historical Background of Unbelief," in *The Culture of Belief*, eds. R. Caporale and A. Grumelli (Berkeley: University of California Press, 1971): 39–52.

25. Edmund Leach, *A Runaway World* (New York: Oxford University Press, 1968), 87.

26. Nolan Pliny Jacobson, *Buddhism: The Religion of Analysis* (Carbondale: Southern Illinois Univdersity Press, 1970), esp. chap. 5.

27. K. Venkata Ramanan, *Nāgārjuna's Philosophy: As Presented in the Mahā-Prajñāpāramitā-Śāstra* (Tokyo: Charles E. Tuttle & Co., 1966), 248.

28. Alfred North Whitehead, *Science and the Modern World* (New York: The Macmillan Co., 1927), 200.

29. Charles Hartshorne, "The Structure of Givenness," *The Philosophical Forum* (1960-1961): 31.

30. Charles Hartshorne, "Personal Identity from A to Z," *Process Studies*, vol. 2, no. 3 (Fall 1972): 213.

31. CPP, vol. 7, par. 571; see also vol. 7, 573-577.

32. Whitehead, "Immortality," *Science and Philosophy*,: 94. (Originally delivered as part of the Ingersoll Lecture at the Harvard Divinity School, April 22, 1941). Erroneous notions like this, however, are as slow to disappear from a nation's life as the weathering of rock, since they serve a social function, in this case to support the irrational "autonomous" nation which tends to insist that whatever is good for the nation is good for all its members. The illusions and compulsions of the supposititious substantial self are now firmly rooted in language, unconscious drives, and widely held social motivations, all of which have been subjected to considerable clinical psychological research. The major terrors of the modern nation are chiefly traceable to this error which sciences such as high energy physics have, as Whitehead says, "completely discarded." Nonetheless, the illusion lives on.

33. Quoted in Louis de la Vallée Poussin, *The Way to Nirvāṇa* (Cambridge: The University Press, 1917), 109.

34. Kenneth K. Inada, personal correspondence, February 16, 1977.

4. Jay McDaniel, *Mahāyāna Enlightenment in Process Perspective*

1. Shin'ichi Hisamatsu, "Ultimate Crisis and Resurrection," Part II, *The Eastern Buddhist*, vol. 8 (October 1975): 64. See also Masao Abe, "Buddhism and Christianity as a Problem of Today," Part II, *Japanese Religions*, vol. 4 (March 1966): 28-31.

2. Alfred North Whitehead, *Process and Reality* (New York: The Macmillian Company, 1929), 230. *Adventures of Ideas* (New York: The Macmillan Company, 1933), 228.

3. Quoted in Keiji Nishitani, "The Standpoint of Śūnyatā," Part I, *The Eastern Buddhist*, vol. 6 (October 1973): 83.

4. Keiji Nishitani, "The Standpoint of Śūnyatā," Part II, *The Eastern Buddhist*, vol. 6 (May 1973): 81ff.

5. Masao Abe, "'Life and Death' and 'Good and Evil' in Zen," *Criterion*, vol. 9 (Autumn 1969): 7ff.

6. See Stephen A. Erickson, *Language and Being, An Analytic Phenomenology* (New Haven: Yale University Press, 1970).

7. Whitehead, *Process and Reaslity*, 375.

8. John B. Cobb, Jr., *A Christian Natural Theology* (Philadelphia: Westminster Press, 1965), 71-79.

9. Whitehead, *Adventures of Ideas*, 266.

10. Hisamatsu, 64.

11. Takao Tanaka, "From a Buddhist Point of View," *John Cobb's Theology in Process*, eds. David Ray Griffin and Thomas J. J. Altizer (Philadelphia: The Westminster Press, 1977), passim.

12. Alfred North Whitehead, *Religion in the Making* (New York: The Macmillan Company, 1926), 141.

5. Kenneth K. Inada, *The American Involvement with Śūnyatā: Prospects*

1. Sarvepalli Radhakrishnan, *Indian Philosophy*, rev. eds. (London: G. Allen and Unwin, 1929, vol. 1 and 1931, vol. 2). These two volumes constitute Radhakrishnan's most influential effort. Volume I contains the lengthy presentation of Buddhism which is slanted towards a Hinduistic metaphysics, for example, on the doctrine of karma and Buddhahood. This is a representative account, however, and there are many works both prior and posterior to it that carry the same slant.

2. 1949 was the year the Second East-West Philosophers' Conference was held in Honolulu, Hawaii under the able direction of Charles A. Moore. It was, in retrospect, probably the best of the five such conferences held there. Convened after World War II, men from the East and West were eager to meet and exchange ideas. Established scholars, such as, S. Radhakrishnan, D. T. Suzuki, Hu Shih and F. S. C. Northrop were present. By then, Northrop had crystallized his singular contribution on East-West methodological differences and emphases in terms of the concepts by intuition and postulation, especially as they appeared in his award-winning book, *The Meeting of East and West* (New York: Macmillan Co., 1946). In the final analysis, the aesthetic and theoretic components correspond with each other and this correspondence he termed, "epistemic correlation." (Ibid., 442–443). Northrop had previously presented the details of his concepts by intuition and postulation in a most original essay, "The Complementary Emphases of Eastern Intuitive and Western Scientific Philosophy." This essay was a paper presented at the First East-West Philosophers' Conference held in Honolulu in 1939 and subsequently published as Chapter 8 in *Philosophy—East and West*, edited by C. A. Moore and published by Princeton University Press, 1946. In this essay Northrop goes into the details of the aesthetic and theoretic components and concludes with three major components of concepts by intuition, i.e., (1) Concept of the Differentiated Aesthetic Continuum, (2) Concept of the Indefinite or Undifferentiated Continuum and (3) Concepts of Differentiations. While the insight into these concepts was very bold and unique, Northrop's overzealousness in tying up Eastern and Western thought and practice ended in gross over-generalization, vagueness and in the end unfruitfulness. Yet there is no denial that his initial insights and bold assertions are still formidable and significant to East-West thought. Future comparative studies could ill-afford to gloss over his contributions.

My personal observation of the 1949 Conference is that the participant's knowledge of the other's field was not commensurate with their eagerness and enthusiasm for the exchange of ideas. Thus the Conference did not generate any real dialogue of East and West and in fact it generated a host of problems. Subsequent conferences have shown marked increase in knowledge of both sectors, but the dialogical nature has yet to develop to an appreciable degree. Some progress is being made, for example, in Buddhist-Christian dialogues but the desideratum is for a more intensifying contact on a broad front that entails both the scientific and humanistic areas. Some fruitful developments have also occurred in the fine and performing arts, but the impact on the general populace is still minuscule.

3. America has now come openly to accept the presence of ethnic forces and to promote their activities. In these, the Asiatic ehtnic groups and their activities invariably reflect a strong Buddhist influence in one way or another.

4. Edward Conze, *Buddhism: Its Essence and Development* (New York: Harper Torchbooks, 1959), 130–131. He was the first Western scholar to call to attention this fascinating nature of *śūnya*.

5. The *ālaya-vijñāna* is literally the "storehouse-consciousness." It contains all empiricistic activities which may start from the perceptual sense faculties but it may also be initiated from itself. In the latter case, it may initiate discriminative activities by sending so-called "memory-seeds" (*bījas*) to be activated in the mind (*manas*). Yet, in the final analysis, the goal is to stop all empiricistic activities in terms of transforming (*parāvritti*) the eight *vijñānas* (eight consciousnesses) into a pure nature of consciousness (*vijñaptimātra*). This is a complex psycho-ontological system of purification, but suffice it to say that in pure consciousness the nature of experience thereafter is characterized by *śūnyatā*.

6. Edward Conze, *Buddhist Wisdom Books* (London: Geo. Allen & Unwin Ltd., 1958). The famous lines from the *Heart Sūtra* read:

Here, O Śāriputra, form is emptiness and the very emptiness is form; emptiness does not differ from form, form does not differ from emptiness; whatever is form, that is emptiness, whatever is emptiness, that is form, the same is true of feelings, perceptions, impulses and consciousness. (p. 81)

The thought revealed here can be taken as the Mahāyāna answer to the *ātman* (self, ego, person, etc.) challenge. In order to demonstrate the *anātman* ("nonself") view, it went into the analysis of the five *skandhas* which are the five constituents of being (*rūpa, vedanā, saṃjñā, saṃskāra, vijñāna*) to exhibit their respective emptiness (*śūnyatā*). Thus ontologically, *ātman=śūnyatā=anātman*.

7. Kenneth K. Inada, *Nāgārjuna, A Translation of his Mūlamadhyamakakārikā* (Tokyo: The Hokuseido Press, 1970), 24.1.

8. Cf. footnote 2.

9. *Mūlamadhyamakakārikā*, 25.19, 20.

10. Ibid., 22.16. In many respects, Nāgārjuna's greatest contribution is to spell out the equation of relational origination and *śūnyatā* in concrete terms. In ordinary perceptual experiences the main emphasis is to capture the *śūnyatā* of such experiences and, vice versa, the understanding of relational origination in its true form will issue forth *śūnyatā*. With *śūnyatā*, everything could exist in the fullest experiential sense. This is the real meaning of the so-called *plenum*

of existence. Indeed, it is a bold assertion on the discovery of an initial epistemological "emptiness" which then opens the way to the ultimate ground of enlightened existence. This is the ground upon which subsequent Mahāyāna schools, such as, T'ien-t'ai, Hua-yen, Pure Land and Zen, will develop.

11. In this connection, Nāgārjuna made a startling statement:

> Whatever is in correspondence with *śūnyatā*, all is in correspondence [i.e., possible].
> Again, whatever is not in correspondence with *śūnyatā*, all is not in correspondence.
>
> *Mūlamadhyamakakārikā*, 24.14.

He was, of course, referring to the state of enlightened existence where the content as well as the so-called "pivot" of experience are lodged in *śūnyatā*.

12. Daisetz T. Suzuki, *Zen and Japanese Culture* (New York; Pantheon Books, Inc., 1959), 357.

6. David Lee Miller, *Buddhism and Wieman on Suffering and Joy*

1. Henry Nelson Wieman, "Intellectual Autobiography," *The Empirical Theology of Henry Nelson Wieman*; ed. Robert W. Bretall, The Library of Living Theology (New York: Macmillan, 1963), 6.

2. Cf. "Wieman's Stature As a Contemporary Theologian," chap. 19, *The Empirical Theology of Henry Nelson Wieman*; 392–397.

3. Henry Nelson Wieman, *Man's Ultimate Commitment* (Carbondale and Edwardsville: Southern Illinois Univ. Press, 1958), 23.

4. Henry Nelson Wieman, *The Source of Human Good* (Chicago: Univ. of Chicago Press, 1946), 57–58.

5. Ibid., 58.

6. Ibid.

7. Wieman, *Man's Ultimate Commitment*, 11.

8. Ibid., 22.

9. Wieman, *The Source of Human Good*, 236.

10. Ibid., 236.

11. Ibid., 241.

12. Ibid.

13. Ibid., 241–242.

14. Ibid., 242.

15. Ibid.

16. Ibid.

17. Ibid., 307.

18. Ibid.

19. Wieman, *Man's Ultimate Commitment*, 305.

20. Ibid., 277.

21. Ibid., 44.

22. Ibid., 276.

23. Ibid.

24. Ibid.

25. Wieman, *The Source of Human Good*, 309.
26. Wieman, *Man's Ultimate Commitment*, 57.
27. Ibid.
28. Ibid., 61.
29. Ibid., 63.
30. Ibid., 62.
31. Ibid., 61.
32. Ibid., 62.
33. Ibid., 23.
34. Ibid., 23–24.
35. Ibid., 24.
36. Ibid.
37. Ibid.
38. Ibid., 25.
39. Ibid.
40. Wieman, *The Source of Human Good*, 106.
41. Ibid., 242.
42. Wieman, *Man's Ultimate Commitment*, 68.
43. Ibid., 278.
44. Ibid.
45. Ibid., 301.
46. Bretall, ed., *Empirical Theology* 3.
47. Ibid., 8–9.
48. Ibid., 3.
49. Wieman, *Man's Ultimate Commitment*, 9.
50. Ibid., 11.
51. Ibid.
52. Ibid., 12.
53. Ibid.
54. For Wieman, God is another word for creativity, creative interchange, creative communication, and creative good.
55. Wieman, *Man's Ultimate Commitment*, 12.
56. Ibid.
57. Ibid., 18.
58. Ibid., 19.
59. Ibid.
60. Ibid.
61. Ibid.
62. Ibid., 20.
63. Ibid., 21.
64. Wieman, *The Source of Human Good*, 181.
65. Ibid., 187.
66. Ibid., 211.
67. Ibid., 212.
68. Ibid., 213.
69. Ibid.
70. Ibid.

71. Ibid., 214.
72. Bretall ed., *Empirical Theology*, 3.
73. Wieman, *Man's Ultimate Commitment*, 167.
74. Ibid.
75. Ibid., 305–306.
76. Bretall, ed., *Empirical Theology*, 388.
77. Ibid.
78. Nolan P. Jacobson, "A Buddhistic-Christian Probe of the Endangered Future," *The Eastern Buddhist*, vol. 15, no. 1 Spring 1982, p. 53.
79. Guy Richard Welbon, *The Buddhist Nirvāṇa and its Western Interpreters* (Chicago: University of Chicago Press, 1968), 304.
80. Herbert Guenther, *Philosophy and Psychology in the Abhidharma* (Berkeley: Shambhala Publications, 1974), 241.
81. Charles Hartshorne, *Creative Synthesis and Philosophic Method* (LaSalle, Illinois: Open Court, 1970), 8.
82. Wieman, *Man's Ultimate Commitment*, 22.
83. Ibid., 23.
84. Nolan P. Jacobson, *Buddhism: The Religion of Analysis* (Carbondale and Edwardsville: Southern Illinois Univ. Press, 1966), 70.
85. Erich Fromm, *To Have or To Be?* (New York: Harper and Row, Publishers, Inc., 1976), 104.
86. Thomas Berry, *Buddhism* (New York: Thomas Y. Crowell Co., 1967), 23.
87. Ibid.
88. Ibid., 23–24.
89. Jacobson, *Buddhism: The Religion of Analysis*, 70.
90. Berry, 24.
91. Wieman, *The Source of Human Good*, 308.
92. Berry, 102.
93. Ibid., 101.
94. Ibid.
95. E. A. Burtt, ed., *The Teachings of the Compassionate Buddha* (New York: The New American Library, 1955), 155.
96. Ibid., 156.
97. Cf. "Living Richly With Dark Realities," chap. 3 in *Man's Ultimate Commitment*, 56–77.
98. Jacobson, *Buddhism: The Religion of Analysis*, 67.
99. Ibid., 70.
100. Ibid., 71.
101. Wieman, *Man's Ultimate Commitment*, 70–71.
102. Ibid., 76.
103. Cf., Burtt, 43–46. The moving parable depicts one Kisa Gotami who gave birth to a boy but when he was just old enough to run and play in the yard, died suddenly. In utter remorse, she carried the dead child on her hip and went from household to household in search of a medicine to revive the child. There was of course no cure for death. She was finally introduced to the Buddha who understood her plight and directed her to collect mustard seeds

from households that have not experienced death. Hard as she tried she could not locate a single household in which death had not occurred, but then suddenly she realized the impermanent nature of things. Accordingly, she brought her dead child to the burning ground for the usual services and regained her peace and tranquillity.

104. Huston Smith, *The Religion of Man* (New York: Harper and Row, 1958), 96.

105. Jacobson, *Buddhism: The Religion of Analysis*, 98.

106. Ibid., 93.

107. Nyanaponika Thera, *The Heart of Buddhist Meditation* (New York: Samuel Weiser, Inc., 1962), 39.

108. Bretall, 4.

109. Ibid., 5.

110. Alfred North Whitehead, *Adventures of Ideas* (New York: Macmillan, 1933), 41.

111. Nolan P. Jacobson, (from unpublished handout in a class entitled, *"Philosopher's Quest in Religion"* at Queen's College, North Carolina, dated September 1976): 3.

112. Ibid.

7. Richard S. Y. Chi, *Buddhist Logic and Western Thought*

1. E. L. Post, "Introduction to a General Theory of Elementary Propositions," *American Journal of Mathematics* 43 (1921): 163–185.

2. Alfred N. Whitehead and Bertrand A. Russell, *Principia Mathematica* 2nd ed. 3 vols. (Cambridge: Cambridge University Press, 1927), xiv.

3. Ibid., xv.

4. Post, 164.

5. Richard S. Y. Chi, *Buddhist Formal Logic* (London: Luzac and Co., Ltd., 1969), xlix-liii.

6. Ibid., xi-xii.

7. St. Stasiak, "Fallacies and Their Classifications According to the Early Hindu Logicians," *Rocznik Orientalistyczny*, vi, 1929, 191–198.

8. Immanuel Kant, *Critique of Pure Reason*, 2nd ed., Eng. trans. N. Kemp Smith (London: Macmillan Co., 1933), viii.

9. J. D. Gergonne, "Essai de dialectique rationelle," *Annales de mathematiques* 7 (1816-7). English trans. William & Martha Kneale, *The Development of Logic* (Oxford: Clarendon Press, 1962), 350.

8. Robert C. Neville, *Buddhism and Process Philosophy*

1. Kenneth K. S. Ch'en recounts the historical encounter of Buddhism and Taoism in his *Buddhism in China* (Princeton: Princeton University Press, 1964),

esp. 48–67. An interesting discussion is to be found in Joseph Needham's *Science and Civilization in CHina*, vol. 2 (Cambridge: Cambridge University Press, 1956), 408–419, where it is argued that Buddhism was responsive to the naturalism of Taoism but that the Buddhists' insistence that impermanence means illusion was rejected by the Taoists and later by the neo-Confucianists. Needham finds the Buddhists' rejection of the world helped to inhibit the development of science in China. As the text below will argue, however, it is not necessary for Buddhism to claim that the world is illusory or that it should be escaped from, even if influential Chinese Buddhist thought and practice claimed just that.

2. See their "A Cross-cultural Approach to the De-Ontological Self Paradigm," *Monist*, vol. 61, no. 1 (1978): 82–95.

3. Process philosophy offers few resources for embodying Buddhism as a transcendental turn, and some reasons for this will be explored here.

4. As a general historical comment, it might be noted that Buddhism prior to the encounter with the West has a certain ranking or set of rankings of what is important in the Buddhist heritage. Responding to Western thought, different things might emerge as important, and what was previously thought to be important may sink toward triviality. This is one of the ways Buddhism changes through encounter. The point of the text is that whereas the epistemological elements are important in responding to the transcendental tradition in the West, conceptions of nature and reality are important in the selective encounter with process philosophy.

5. A straightforward, clear analysis of the ancient agreements and disagreements is to be found in Edward Conze's *Buddhist Thought in India* (Ann Arbor, Mich.: University of Michigan Press, 1967), 134–158.

6. I will try to make this presentation of process philosophy general enough to apply to all or most of those who have been decisively influenced by Whitehead's theory of causation by prehension. Whitehead's own central text, of course, is *Process and Reality* (New York: Macmillan, 1929). The classic analysis of it is William Christian's *An Interpretation of Whitehead's Metaphysics* (New Haven: Yale University Press, 1959). An extraordinary new commentary is Elizabeth M. Kraus's *The Metaphysics of Experience: A Companion to Whitehead's Process and Reality* (New York: Fordham University Press, 1979).

There is a significant disagreement among process philosophers as to whether the loss of subjective immediacy with the attainment of "satisfaction" is very significant; although I claim that it is, and reflect this in the exposition below, Hartshorne and his followers claim that it is not; see Hartshorne's discussion in *Creative Synthesis and Philosophic Method* (LaSalle, Ill.: Open Court, 1970), 118, passim. My own special developments of the process philosophy of nature are to be found in *The Cosmology of Freedom* (New Haven: Yale University Press, 1974), pts. 1–2.

7. For an analysis of Whitehead's relation to the Western tradition see Charles Hartshorne and William L. Reese's *Philosophers Speak of God* (Chicago: University of Chicago Press, 1953).

8. David A. Dilworth calls Whitehead's metaphysics "probably the most sustained philosophical articulation of the conception of reality as process in

either Eastern or Western traditions," in his "Whitehead's Process Realism, the Abhidharma Dharma Theory, and the Mahāyāna Critique," *International Philosophical Quarterly*, vol. 18, no. 2 (June, 1978): 152.

9. Thomas J. J. Altizer, "The Buddhist Ground of the Whiteheadian God," *Process Studies* 5/4 (Winter, 1975): 230; Dilworth.

10. Whitehead, *Process and Reality*, 30.

11. Dilworth: *op. cit.* 155; Whitehead, 28.

12. Dilworth's analysis is dependent in part on a paper by Justus Buchler, "On a Strain of Arbitrariness in Whitehead's System," *The Journal of Philosophy*, vol. 66 (1969): 589–600. Buchler maintains a doctrine of "ontological parity," to the effect that anything that is real is just as real as anything else. The "arbitrary strain" he criticized in Whitehead is that for the latter, some things are more important or interesting than others, but Buchler did not distinguish between degrees of reality and degrees of value.

13. Dilworth directs his argument against the alleged ultimacy of actual occasions. But perhaps Whitehead's eternal objects could be said to have "own being." Yet Whitehead said that apart from God's primordial envisionment of them, eternal objects are completely indeterminate; so they cannot have "own being" in *that* sense. Perhaps then they have "own being" as graded possibilities in the divine vision. But then their determinate reality depends on divine envisioning decision and the "own being" would have to be derivative from God's "own being." Whitehead was not consistent regarding his theory of God and the claim that God must exemplify the characteristics of actual occasions. If God does the latter, then God too is temporal and has no "own being." If God does indeed have "own being" of primordial conceptuality, that is a mystery otherwise unrelated to Whitehead's account of process. For an attempt to reach a satisfactory doctrine for Whitehead, see Lewis S. Ford's "Whitehead's Categoreal Derivation of Divine Existence," *Monist* 54/3 (July, 1970), 374–400, and his "Neville on the One and the Many," *Southern Journal of Philosophy* vol. 10, no. 1 (Spring, 1972): 79–84.

14. Dilworth follows Conze, in *Buddhism: Its Essence and Development* (New York: Harper, 1959), 130, in noting that the root meaning of *śūnya*, "empty," is "swollen," from the root *svi*.

15. *Mūlamadhyamakakārikā*, 24.9, trans. Frederick J. Streng, *Emptiness: A Study in Religious Meaning* (Nashville: Abingdon Press, 1967), 213.

16. A subtle discussion of this is to be found in William Johnston's *The Still Point: Reflections on Zen and Christian Mysticism* (New York: Fordham University Press, 1970).

17. Streng, 139–146.

18. Dilworth, 162–163.

19. Ibid., 167–169.

20. Dilworth's approach reflects a Kantian and neo-Kantian interpretation of paradigms. I have criticized this at length in "Specialties and Worlds," *Hastings Center Studies*, vol. 2, no. 1 (January, 1974).

21. See the magnificent first chapter of Whitehead's *Process and Reality*.

22. Nāgārjuna, 1.4 beginning at p. 183.

23. Ibid., 1.5–6.

24. Ibid., 1.7.
25. Ibid., 1.8.
26. Ibid., 1.9.
27. Ibid., 1.10.
28. Ibid., 1.11.
29. Ibid., 1.12.
30. Ibid., 1.14.
31. Streng, 167.
32. Altizer, 235f.
33. Ibid., 230.
34. See *Process and Reality*, 374f., 443, 124; on 94f., Whitehead said, "this doctrine of organism is the attempt to describe the world as a process of generation of individual actual entities, each with its own absolute self-attainment. This concrete finality of the individual is nothing else than a decision referent beyond itself. The 'perpetual perishing' of individual absoluteness is thus foredoomed. But the 'perishing' of absoluteness is the attainment of 'objective immortality.' . . . Continuity concerns what is potential; whereas actuality is incurably atomic. . . . So far as physical relations are concerned, contemporary events happen in *causal* independence of each other. . . . The contemporary world is in fact divided and atomic, being a multiplicity of definite actual entities. These contemporary actual entities are divided from each other, and are not themselves divisible into other contemporary actual entities."
35. Garma C. C. Chang, *The Buddhist Teaching of Totality: The Philosophy of Hwa Yen Buddhism* (University Park, Pa.: The Pennsylvania State University Press, 1971), 122f.
36. Ibid., 156.
37. Francis H. Cook, *Hua-yen Buddhism: The Jewel Net of Indra* (University Park, Pa.: The Pennsylvania State University Press, 1977), 73.
38. Ibid., 112. The Fa-tsang text is his Treatise, *Hua-yen i-ch'eng chiao i fen-ch'i chang*, translated by Cook from the *Taisho* edition, vol. 45, no. 1866; this passage is at 489b.
39. Ibid., 115f.
40. Hartshorne, 198.
41. I have argued this thesis extensively in *The Cosmology of Freedom*, chaps. 1–6.
42. Chang, 156.
43. This theory is developed at length in my *God the Creator* (Chicago: University of Chicago Press, 1968), Part 1, and supplemented in *The Cosmology of Freedom*, chap. 2, and *Soldier, Sage, Saint* (New York: Fordham University Press, 1978), chaps. 3–5.
44. The difficulty with Whitehead's philosophical theology is that he still proceeded to treat God only cosmologically.

Selected Bibliography

Books

Ames, Van Meter. *Zen and American Thought*. Honolulu: University of Hawaii Press, 1962.

Chi, Richard S.Y. *Buddhist Formal Logic*. London: Luzac and Co., Ltd., 1969.

Govinda, Lama Anagarika. *The Psychological Attitude of Early Buddhist Philosophy*. London: Rider & Company, 1961.

Guenther, Herbert V. *Philosophy and Psychology in the Abhidharma*. Berkeley: Shambhala Publications, 1974.

Hall, David L. *The Civilization of Experience*. New York: Fordham University Press, 1973.

Hartshorne, Charles. *Creative Synthesis and Philosophic Method*. Lanham, Maryland: University Press of America, Inc., 1983.

———. *Insights & Oversights of Great Thinkers*. Albany: State University of New York Press, 1983.

Inada, Kenneth K., ed. *East-West Dialogues in Aesthetics*. Buffalo: Council on International Studies, SUNY at Buffalo, 1978.

———. *Nāgārjuna: A Translation of His Mūlamadhyamakakārikā with an Introductory Essay*. Tokyo: Hokuseido Press, 1970, 1975.

Izutsu, Toshihiko. *Toward a Philosophy of Zen Buddhism*. Boulder: Prajna Press, 1982.

Jacobson, Nolan Pliny. *Buddhism and the Contemporary World*. Carbondale: Southern Illinois University Press, 1983.

———. *Buddhism: the Religion of Analysis*. Carbondale: Southern Illinois University Press, 1966, 1970.

Jayatilleke, K.N. *Early Buddhist Theory of Knowledge*. London: George Allen & Unwin Ltd., 1963.

Kraus, Elizabeth M. *The Metaphysics of Experience*. New York: Fordham University Press, 1979.

McDermott, John J. *The Culture of Experience*. New York: New York University Press, 1976.

Moore, Charles A., ed. *Philosophy—East and West*. Princeton: Princeton University Press, 1946.

————. *Essays in East-West Philosophy*. Honolulu: University of Hawaii Press, 1951.

————. *Philosophy and Culture: East and West*. Honolulu: University of Hawaii Press, 1962.

————. *The Status of the Individual in East and West*. Honolulu: University of Hawaii Press, 1968.

Murti, T.R.V. *The Central Philosophy of Buddhism*. London: George Allen & Unwin Ltd., 1955.

Nakamura, Hajime. *Parallel Developments: A Comparative History of Ideas*. Tokyo & New York: Kodansha, 1975.

Neville, Robert C. *Reconstruction of Thinking*. Albany: State University of New York Press, 1981.

————. *The Tao and the Daimon*. Albany: State University of New York Press, 1982.

Nishitani, Keiji. *Religion and Nothingness*. Berkeley: University of California Press, 1982.

Northrop, F.S.C. *The Meeting of East and West*. New York: The MacMillan Company, 1946.

Odin, Steve. *Process Metaphysics and Hua-yen Buddhism*. Albany: State University of New York Press, 1982.

Peirce, Charles Sanders. *Collected Papers of Charles Sanders Peirce*. Vols. 1–6 edited by Charles Hartshorne and Paul Weiss. Vols. 7, 8 edited by A.W. Burke. Cambridge, Mass.: Harvard University Press, 1931–1935, 1958.

Rahula, Walpole. *What the Buddha Taught*. New York: Grove Press, Inc., 1974.

Ramanan, Venkata K. *Nāgārjuna's Philosophy: As Presented in the Mahā-prajñāpāramitā-śāstra*. Rutland: Charles E. Tuttle Company Inc., 1966.

Sangharakshita, Bhikshu. *A Survey of Buddhism*. Boulder: Shambhala Publications, 1978.

Schilpp, Paul Arthur, ed. *The Philosophy of Alfred North Whitehead*. New York: Tudor Publishing Company, 1951.

Schinzinger, Robert, translated and introduced. *Nishida: Intelligibility and the Philosophy of Nothingness*. Westport: Greenwood Press, 1973.

Stcherbatsky, Theodore. *The Conception of Buddhist Nirvāna*. With comprehensive analysis and introduction by Jaideva Singh. Delhi: Motilal Banarsidass, 1977.

Suzuki, Daisetz Teitaro. *Essays in Zen Buddhism*. First, Second and Third Series. London: Rider & Co., 1953.

Whitehead, Alfred North. *Adventures of Ideas*. New York: Macmillan Company, 1933.

————. *Modes of Thought*. New York: Macmillian Company, 1938.

————. *Process and Reality*. Corrected edition edited by David Ray Griffin and Donald W. Sherburne. New York: Free Press, 1978.

————. *Science and the Modern World*. New York: Macmillan Company, 1948.

Wieman, Henry Nelson. *Man's Ultimate Commitment*. Carbondale: Southern Illinois University Press, 1958.

————. *The Source of Human Good*. Chicago: University of Chicago Press, 1946.

Yampolsky, Philip B., trans. *The Platform Sutra of the Sixth Patriarch*. New York: Columbia University Press, 1967.

Journals

Many stimulating articles of intercultural nature, exchange and synthesis appear each year in the learned journals of the world. Rather than listing them all, the editors would like to recommend the following prominent journals that carry a continuing dialogue on Buddhist and Western thought.

Philosophy East & West
Eastern Buddhist
Journal of Buddhist Philosophy
Journal of Chinese Philosophy
Journal of Indian Philosophy
Journal of the International Association for Buddhist Studies.
Process Studies
Darshana

Index

Abhidhamma, Abhidharma, 105, 124
Actual occasions, actual entities, 124–25
Adams, Henry, viii
Adhipateya, Adhipati-pratyaya (dominant condition), 148
Aesthetic creativity in Chinese art, 26–29
Aesthetic experience, 19–20, 26–30, 40–42; communicates mystical depth, not union, 26; confusion of term "ineffable," 26–27
Aesthetic foundations of life, x, 41–42
Aesthetics, viii, 25–28; aesthetic of interrelatedness in Buddhism and Whitehead, 132–34, 139–40
Afghanistan, 37
Ālaya-vijñāna (receptacle of being), 81
Allport, Gordon, xv
Altizer, Thomas J. J., 123, 132–34; on Nāgārjuna, 133; view of Whitehead, 133–34
American Oriental Society, viii
American philosophy, vii, viii, xi, xii, xiii–xvi; primary responsibility of, 14, 18–20; pursuit of novel Oriental evidence, 20, 28–35
American pragmatism: deeply embedded in American people, 72–76; initial emphasis on holistic nature of experience lost, 76; opted toward science and its methodology, 76
American propensity for śūnyatā experience, xiv; Asian Studies in American higher education, 73; exposure to Asiatic thought, 71–73;

fluidity of American culture, 73–74; helped by recent interchange of scholars, 72–73; opportunity to understand Buddhism limited until now, 71–72
Anattā, Anātman (denial of bifurcating substantial self), 4, 52–53; definition of, xv, 12; non-substantialism, 83. See also Bifurcating self; Self; Self-encapsulated culture; self-encapsulated individuals; Selfhood; self-interest; selflessness of Buddhism
Anglo-European culture: basic processes of, 15, 23; contrasted with Chinese, 25–26; its constricted mentality, 33–35; possible contributions from aesthetic and mystical sensibilities of the Chinese, 26–35
Archery: grounded in śūnyatā, 85
Aristotle, xii, 4, 24, 115, 118, 148
Association for Asian Studies, viii
Asymmetrical relations, xiii, 1, 9, 120, 134, 139
Ātman-view (substantialism), 83
Avatamsaka Sūtra, 135
Avijjāsava (ignorance), xvii

Basic religious problem: capacity to undergo radical transformation and awareness of original experience underlying all conventionalized ways, 91–94
Beauty, xii, 12–13, 25–28, 65–66, 105–06. See also Aesthetic experience

RELATED TITLES FROM SUNY PRESS

Process Metaphysics and Hua-Yen Buddhism. Steve Odin

The Tao and the Daimon. Robert C. Neville

Insights and Oversights of the Great Thinkers: An Evaluation of Western Philosophy. Charles Hartshorne

A Mongolian Living Buddha: Biography of the Kanjurwa Khutughtu. Paul Hyer and Sechin Jagchid

Buddhist Faith and Sudden Enlightenment. Sung-Bae Park

Perspective in Whitehead's Metaphysics. Stephen David Ross

The Spirit of American Philosophy. John E. Smith

Reconstruction of Thinking. Robert C. Neville